GRAMMAR
For Those Who Missed It in High School

GRAMMAR
For Those Who Missed It in High School

Robert Stanton and Frederic Weekes

iUniverse, Inc.
Bloomington

GRAMMAR For Those Who Missed It in High School

iUniverse books may be ordered through booksellers or by contacting:

iUniverse
1663 Liberty Drive
Bloomington, IN 47403
www.iuniverse.com
1-800-Authors (1-800-288-4677)

ISBN: 978-1-4759-4152-4 (sc)
ISBN: 978-1-4759-4153-1 (ebk)

Printed in the United States of America

iUniverse rev. date: 08/21/2012

CONTENTS

INTRODUCTION

This book is a guide to finding the power inherent in language, power which is diminished in the estimation of listeners and readers when errors in English are present. By reading this text, writers, speakers, students, professionals and all others who wish to express their ideas clearly will become aware of the errors that they have been making in the course of their work.

This is not an attempt to write a book on grammar or a text on style. The purpose is to present a compilation of errors made frequently in conversation and in writing. The errors listed here come mostly from bureaucrats, journalists, newscasters, and politicians. It is from their utterances and writings that this material has been gathered during the past three years. The identity of the individuals whose writings and conversations are cited is not disclosed. Indeed, many of the citations are altered slightly in order to hide their origin.

It is acknowledged by students of the language that there are several levels in usage, from formal English to English spoken in the gymnasium. All of us should feel free to vary the level of language in use to suit the requirements of communications, just as we are free to change clothes according to social circumstances. Language, after all, is but the clothing of thought. A master or mistress of the English language is the person who knows and can practice appropriately all the levels of usage. As an example, speakers and writers must know and practice the use of formal English in situations that require it: the courtroom, the editorial page, the job interview, the keynote address and the formal dinner party. Most educated people will find themselves using formal English if they cease and desist in making the errors listed in this text.

The tendency in America today is to relax the standards of speech, dress, and manners with result that informal English is in use, on occasion, in formal circumstances. The attempt is made here to persuade readers that the level of formality should match or exceed the requirements of the situation. Formal situations require the use of formal English: English spoken and written without errors. In today's mode of relaxed codes, it should be noted that, like it or not, we are not judged so much by our demeanor as by how we speak.

Readers should be comforted in the knowledge that the outpourings of bureaucrats, journalists, newscasters, politicians and the rest of us were read and listened to until it was no longer possible to identify additional errors committed commonly by educated people. At the end of the search, continued reading and listening turned up variations on errors noted previously, never errors not observed before.

The errors that have been collected and compiled into this text are placed in four categories. There does not seem to be any arrangement or grouping of the errors that reveals a truth or commonality about them. Errors are errors, and they tend to appear in all usages of the language. The errors are arranged in part alphabetically and in part in categories such as NOUNS AND OTHER WORDS, and VERBS.

Verbs are listed first. Adverbs come next. There are ten sets of mistakes in the third category called NOUNS AND OTHER WORDS. In the fourth category, called MISCELLANEOUS STUFF, all the remaining odd-ball errors are gathered, errors that defy being placed in separate categories, everything from the overuse of the adverb 'basically' to the significance of running across 'what' in sentences in which other words and constructions are preferred.

Under EDITING, sentences in their original form are presented so that readers may arm themselves with blue pencils and edit them to taste.

The ANTHOLOGY contains the works of six authors, Ulysses Grant to Leo Tolstoy. These are presented for readers' pleasure as well as for purposes of demonstrating that great writers do not commit the common errors that are the subject of this book.

The book ends with a brief CONCLUSION.

VERBS

DEBUT, PLATEAU and PREMIER

'Debut' is a French word meaning 'beginning.' Years ago we used the word to describe the presentation to society of a young woman, as in "Catherine Smithers made her debut at the Country Club Saturday night at a dinner-dance given by her parents." Later, writers for the electronic industry, thirsting for a short word to describe the introduction of a new product, drafted 'debut.' It is coincidental that the coming-out party was in decline.

Companies started to 'debut' new computers, new oscilloscopes and new radar sets. The word had made the transition from French noun to transitive American verb. So far, so good, although marginal. On occasion, however, writers were required to use 'debut', the verb, in the past tense. Hello, trouble. It becomes 'debutted,' and the writers hoped that the readers understood that it would be pronounced 'deb-you-ed. The first time many of us read about a computer that had 'debutted,' we thought it had lost its derrière. Stick with, "ABC Company has introduced its new, super-galactic number cruncher at the trade show in Las Vegas." Goodbye and good riddance to 'debutted.' Hello, 'introduced.'

As we discuss French nouns that have become transitive verbs in our language, let us not forget 'plateau' and 'premier.' It is acceptable to say that hikers reached the plateau without oxygen, but to say that the sales curve 'plateaued' last quarter, WOW! For 'plateaued,' say 'reached its peak.' One may say that a certain movie had its premier last week, but to say that it 'premiered' last week, double WOW! The French do not like Franglais. We ought not to speak Englench.

GERUND

Verbals (verb forms) are not always used as verbs. Some verbals can be used as a noun or an adjective. When a verbal ends with -ing and is used as a noun, it is called a gerund.

Traveling, like reading, broadens the mind.

What does "used as a noun" mean? It means that the verbal is used as a person, place or thing; it's used as a subject of another verb or the object of a verb or a preposition. In the example above, "Traveling" is the subject of "broadens," and "reading" is the object of "like." Because they also end in -ing, they are gerunds.

When a name, a noun, or a pronoun is written before a gerund, formal usage requires that the modifier (the word before the gerund) be possessive:

No one told me about John's leaving.
(not "about John leaving")

His being here is a mystery.
(not "Him being here . . .")

This is the 40th anniversary of KCTN's providing television
services. (not "of KCTN providing")

He was able to leave town by train without their noticing.
(not "without them noticing")

There are signs of France's seeking a close relationship
with Great Britain once more. (not "of France seeking")

When a verbal ends in -ing but is not used as a noun, a noun before it is not possessive. In the sentence "Who is the <u>man painting</u> the house?" the word "painting" is not used as a noun; it's used as an adjective to modify "man." So there's no need to write "man's."

Here are two more sentences in which nouns are not possessive because the -ing verbals following them are not used as nouns:

It being Sunday, I am not working.
My work being finished, I went to bed.

In each of these sentences, the word preceding the comma form an "Absolute Construction." Notice that these words almost form sentences: "It was Sunday," "My work was finished." But instead of a verb, each has a participle, "being." These don't function as nouns, so they're not gerunds, and so there's no need for "It" or "work" to be a possessive.

If you don't want to deal with things like absolute constructions, you can replace each of these sentences with a simpler version:

I do not work on Sunday.
I went to bed after my work was finished.

TO GET

The verb <u>to get</u> receives a thorough workout from us every day. We cannot get out of bed without using it. The dictionary guides us in finding some of the uses for this verb, and it is a simple matter to think of others. Here is a partial list.

Get ready, get even, get hurt, get up, get down, get to go along, get a reputation, get the better of, get sick, get your luggage, get your feet wet, get to sleep, get rich, get into trouble, get after them, get ahead, get around, get wind of, get with it, get at, get away with, get cracking, get your goat, get somewhere, get through, get together, get off my back, get on with it, get going, get tough, and get lost.

If one can find an alternative to the overused verb, <u>to get</u>, that does not sound stilted, use it. One of the marks of speaking and writing well is the avoidance of repetition; another is the use of the words that convey the exact meaning intended while remaining within the common knowledge of most people.

Some examples of substitutions for <u>to get</u> are as follows:

<u>Prepare</u> for get ready
<u>Arise</u> for get up
<u>Accompany</u> for get to go along
<u>Earn</u> a reputation for getting one
<u>Overcome</u> for get the better of
<u>Find your bags</u> for get your luggage
<u>Find out about</u> for get wind of
<u>Get lost</u> for get lost (difficult to improve on)

GOING, MUST and WILL

The two words "gonna" (going to) and "gowin" (going) are both derivatives of the verb "to go" but have distinct meanings.

"Gonna" means intention or future action. Intention: "I'm gonna vote this year." Future action: "I'm gonna deposit this check in the bank."

"Gowin" means motion or direction: "After work I'm gowin home; where you gowin?"

"Gonna" invades the conversation of otherwise well-spoken individuals on radio and television. The performers who appear nightly, and even those who appear on Sundays only, might ease the pain on listeners by reducing the number of times they say "gonna." As alternatives use "will" and "plan to" to indicate future action, as in "How do you plan to vote?" and "Will you be attending the convention?" What a relief!

In either writing or speaking, the "-ing" spelling (as in "going") can be retained, but with occasional inefficiencies. One of them is "going to have to:" "To be competitive, New York is going to have to lower its taxes." This is perfectly grammatical English but lacks the punch of "To be competitive, New York must lower its taxes." If the future is intended, "will" is efficient: "To be competitive, New York will be required to lower its taxes."

TO LAY and TO LIE

Lay means to put on or beat down as in, "lay waste," and to bury as in, "lay to rest." Comedians lay eggs. Hens lay eggs. The verb lay takes a direct object. The verb lie does not. Lie means to assume a horizontal position, as in, "lie down." An hour is required to read all the uses of both words.

The confusion between the two words arises because the past tense of lie is lay, as in, "when he lay down to sleep". Recommendation: memorize the principal parts, or use other words, or return to this page. Here are a few defective sentences to illustrate incorrect usage in these verb forms.

1. I need to lay down and sleep for a week. (Should be lie.)
2. I found this book laying on the table. It was laying in that corner. I think it had been laying there for a week. (Should be lying in all three sentences.)
3. It has laid there for a week. (Should be lain.)

Here are the principal parts for to lay and to lie.

Infinitive	to lay an egg	to lie in bed
Present	I lay an egg now	I lie in bed now
Past	I laid an egg yesterday	I lay in bed yesterday
Present participle	I am laying an egg	I am lying in bed
Past participle	I have laid an egg	I have lain in bed

PLURALS

We know that <u>one</u> of anything is singular and <u>two</u> or more of anything represents the plural. We were taught to say "There <u>is</u> one dog," and "There are <u>two</u> dogs." In the last decade, plural has hopped out the window. Singular has taken over. Paying no attention to quantities involved, many Americans now say, "There's three choices," or "There's two days left." All protestations notwithstanding, "there's" is a contraction of "there is" and therefore is the singular form of the verb. No amount of entreaty will persuade a listener who hears "there's" that the speaker meant "there are."

The incorrect use of the singular in place of the plural has become so prevalent that the few Americans who still use the plural correctly could live in a new town in the desert of eastern Oregon and remain undetected. We could call the town Pluritania.

Growing up was more hazardous early in the past century than it is now. Saying "there <u>is</u> two" was an offense punishable by writing "There <u>are</u> two" fifty times on the blackboard while schoolmates were outside playing.

Distinguishing between "there's" and "there are" is not the only challenge facing us in the use of the plural. There are also collective nouns, such as "group," "number," "cluster," "family" and "bunch." Following one of these collective nouns, is it proper to use the singular or plural form of the verb? Is it "A group of ducks <u>were</u> in the way," or "A group of ducks <u>was</u> in the way"? What about "A number of people has/have complained about this," or "The number of applications has/have been surprising"? And what about pronouns? Can you write "The steering committee <u>has</u> met and decided that <u>they</u> want more information," "has" being singular and "they" being plural?

To begin with, the rules for the word "number" are special. If you write "a number," use a plural verb (A number of people <u>have</u> complained about this"). If you write "<u>the</u> number," use a singular verb ("The number of applications <u>has</u> been surprising").

With other collective nouns, if the noun refers to a commodity, something that isn't countable, use the singular form of the verb ("A fraction of the water <u>has</u> spilled into the basement"). If the collective noun refers to two or more individual items, use the plural form of the verb ("Our people are tired of waiting").

Sometimes a collective noun may be used with either a singular or plural verb, depending on whether the noun refers to its group as a unit or to its members as individuals:

A. Collective noun referring to its group as a unit:
    "Our group <u>is</u> ready to act."

B. Collective nouns referring to its members as individuals:
    "Our group <u>have</u> been arriving all evening."

In cases such as this, it is the writer's decision whether to use a singular or plural verb. But having made the election of singular or plural verb, the writer must remain consistent in number, including pronouns, for the remainder of the paragraph.

One can avoid using a collective noun on occasion by saying, as an example, "many ducks were in the way" instead of "a group of ducks were in the way."

SPLIT INFINITIVES

Splitting infinitives, such as <u>to eat</u> or <u>to walk</u>, by placing a word (usually an adverb) between <u>to</u> and the verb risks losing power. Instead of saying "to quickly eat" or "to slowly walk," say "to eat quickly" or "to walk slowly."

Here are more examples of an infinitive split by an adverb:

> To <u>first</u> go through inspection
> To <u>aggressively</u> invest in small companies
> To <u>fully</u> use one's prestige

The phrases have more punch with the adverbs placed after the verb than they do with the adverb splitting the infinitive.

> To go through inspection first
> To invest in small companies aggressively
> To use one's prestige fully

Let us examine some examples of split infinitives, determine the resulting imprecision, and suggest remedies.

A.   Don't split an infinitive with a comparative.

Do not split an infinitive with an adverb such as <u>better</u>, as in "to better serve you" and "to better acquaint you with the organization." When a comparative such as <u>better</u>, <u>longer</u> or <u>older</u> is used, the comparative, whenever possible, should be followed by the word <u>than</u> and an explanation. Here are examples: <u>better</u> than mom's pie, <u>longer</u> than from here to the moon, and <u>older</u> than anyone at this party. In place of "to better serve you" say "to serve you better than before." In place of "to better acquaint you with the organization," say "to acquaint you with the organization better than ever."

Do not split the infinitive in the first place. When a comparative is used, add <u>than</u> and an explanation.

If the people who say "to better serve you" mean to say "to serve you better than ever before," or "to serve you better than last year," then they should say it. Or when they say "to better acquaint you with our organization," and they mean to say "to acquaint you with our organization more thoroughly than previously," then they should say that.

B.   Don't split an infinitive and cause ambiguity.

Here is a sentence that has been rendered unclear by splitting the infinitive with <u>at least</u>. "Democrats want to at least impose a six-year term limit on powerful committee chairmen." Does <u>at least</u> in the sentence above mean that the Democrats are considering a shorter term limit than six years on committee chairmen, or does it mean that they (the Democrats) have in mind other tortures than term limits for committee chairman? Let us move <u>at least</u> so that infinitive <u>to impose</u> is not split. Now the sentence reads "The Democrats want to impose at least a six years term limit on powerful committee chairmen." Now we see that Democrats are limiting their revenge on committee chairmen to term limits.

Having injected some clarity by un-splitting the infinitive, we can achieve complete clarity by a final rewrite: "Democrats want to impose a term limit of no more than six years on the chairmanship of powerful committee chairmen." Note that it is necessary to indicate that the term limit is on the chairmanship and not on the congressman's entire career in the House of Representatives.

C.   Don't split an infinitive with an adverb in a sentence that has two verbs.

" . . . to accurately measure and assign values to samples . . ." In this sentence, we have an infinitive that is split by an adverb, two verbs that may be modified by one adverb, and confused readers. Does <u>accurately</u>

modify both <u>measure</u> and <u>assign</u>, or just <u>measure</u>? We may never know, but if the infinitive is not split, there is no question. Here is the sentence re-written: " . . . to measure accurately and assign value to samples . . ." When the infinitive is not split, it is clear that <u>accurately</u> modifies the verb <u>measure</u>, and not the verb <u>assign</u>.

D.   Don't split an infinitive when there is no need to.

"There is no consensus on how to substantively restructure police departments in America." As <u>substantively</u> adds little to the meaning of the sentence, it can be written, "There is no consensus on how to restructure police departments in America."

"Many business people do not want the idea to even get that far." Without the split infinitive, the sentence reads "Many business people do not want the idea to get even that far."

Taking care not to split infinitives may be viewed as inconsequential but each step taken toward error-free English, whether in writing or conversation, results in using the standard form of the King's English. We appear to be competent speakers and writers if we prevent errors, no matter how small, from creeping into our communications.

SUBJUNCTIVES

We use the subjunctive mode when expressing a wish, a volition, or the combination of a condition and a thought contrary to fact. Here is an example of each, with the subjunctive in capitals.

A. Expressing a wish

She wishes she WERE in Germany (Not WAS)

B. Expressing a volition

I insist that he WALK to church. (Not WALKS)

C. The condition (if) and a thought contrary to fact

If this WERE Friday, I could go skiing. (Not WAS)

Here the subjunctive is used because the ability to go skiing is conditional on the day's being Friday and the speaker knows that it is not Friday but some other day. It would be wrong to say, "If this WAS Friday . . . ." The condition is contrary to fact. What does "contrary to fact" mean? It means that the speaker knows that the condition does not exist.

On the other hand, say the skier has lost track of the day of the week. He does not know whether it is Friday. Then it would be correct to say, "If this IS Friday, I can go skiing." Here, the day's being Friday is not contrary to fact. It's just unknown, so the subjunctive is not used.

Here is a second example. "If he were alive, he would be eighty-four years old today." (You know he is not alive—it's contrary to fact—so use the subjunctive WERE). On the other hand, when you do not know whether he is alive—there is nothing contrary to fact in the sentence—use the present tense IS. "If he is alive, he is eighty-four years old today."

ADVERBS

There are dozens of rules concerning the use of adverbs. We limit our interest in the use of adverbs to three suggestions. First suggestion: use the adverb only when it adds meaning to the sentence. Although that concept appears elementary, writers and speakers use adverbs when no adverb is called for. Our second suggestion: use the adverb that adds the correct meaning. Imprecise adverbs confuse readers. Our third suggestion: try to place the adverb after the verb. We recognize that this is not possible in all sentences, but it is worth a try.

A. Use an adverb only when it adds meaning to the sentence.

Here are several examples of sentences containing adverbs that add no meaning and only clutter the sentences. These sentences contain more power with the adverbs removed than they do with the adverbs left in.

A. The company would clearly be better off producing toys rather than computers.

B. He is a person whom I actually rather like.

C. If we were truly to advance the cause of liberty . . .

D. We are interested in the changes that the Democrats will really offer this year.

E. He was noticeably less talkative.

F. If the Republicans are effectively allowed to choose Jim Smith's successor . . .

G. His record-setting run in the 100-meter dash received relatively few headlines.

H. I believe there is something basically unhealthy about swimming at that beach.

I. Even after finally adjusting for high altitude . . .

J. The technology does not currently exist.

K. Specifically, the minister's economic plan is designed to tackle one of the state's greatest obstacles to growth: excessive red tape.

L. To truly put the deficit issue behind him, the governor must present a credible plan.

M. He has the authority to totally disregard all the information.

N. Adams remains <u>arguably</u> the only candidate with a chance of winning.

There are times when adverbs are required to convey the meaning intended. We include two sentences whose adverbs (underlined) add meaning. We wish to demonstrate that we are not anti-adverb.

A. She runs <u>very</u> quickly.

B. He gives a speech <u>effortlessly</u>.

B.   Use the adverb that adds the correct meaning.

Imprecise adverbs are used in the four sentences that follow:

A. "When the raccoon came the following night, he scratched <u>adorably</u> on the glass. (Raccoons know nothing about <u>adorably</u>. The viewer thought the scene was adorable.

B. "I lay <u>vacantly</u> on the sofa for a while . . ." (Let us allow that a person can be on a sofa with a vacant mind. It is doubtful that one could have lain vacantly.)

C. "Justice Oliver W. Holmes once <u>famously</u> said of Franklin D. Roosevelt that he had a second-class intellect but a first-class temperament." (Justice Holmes did not speak famously. His remark about the president became famous.)

D. " . . . the concept of critical thinking which asserts that children should be able to digest and analyze what they learn rather than <u>traditionally</u> memorizing their lessons." (Memorizing lessons may be the traditional method of learning. One cannot memorize traditionally.)

C.   Try to place the adverb after the verb.

If you can place the adverb after the verb without wrecking the meaning of the sentence, do so. Here are two sentences whose meanings are clear with the adverb in the middle of the verb, sentences in which the adverb adds meaning, but nevertheless two sentences that are more powerful when the adverb is placed after the verb rather than when it is placed before or in the middle of the verb.

A.   People are <u>bitterly</u> complaining about the lack of soap.

B.   He was <u>savagely</u> attacked by other members of the Senate.

The power of the sentences above is contained in the adverbs. If the adverbs remain in the middle of the verbs, as they are written above, much of the power in these sentences is lost. In sentence A above, the reader or listener wants to read or hear the action (<u>are</u> <u>complaining</u>), followed by the style, (<u>bitterly</u>) and finally the reason (<u>the</u> <u>lack of</u> <u>soap</u>). So A above should read "People are complaining <u>bitterly</u> about the lack of soap." And B above, for the same reasons, should read "He was attacked <u>savagely</u> by other members of the Senate."

In most instances, the position near the end of the sentence is the position of power. A rough-and-ready guide to structuring sentences with power is to put the most important part at or toward the end, the next most important part at or toward the beginning, and all the junk in the middle.

NOUNS AND OTHER WORDS

MEANINGS OF A FEW WORDS
MISPRONOUNCED WORDS
MISSPELLED WORDS
NEWSPEAK WORDS
NON-EXISTENT WORDS
NOUNS AS ADJECTIVES
PHYSICAL DIMENSIONS
POPULAR WORDS
REDUNDANCIES
WEST COAST WORDS

MEANINGS OF A FEW WORDS

Although and While
Use the word "While" to mean only "the time that," as in "While I was in college, I worked as a musician." Don't use "While" to mean "in spite of the fact that," as in "While I went to college, I don't consider myself to be well educated." Say, "Although I went to college, I don't consider myself well educated."

Among and Between
Use "Between" when discussing two of anything as in "The difference between Charles and me . . ." and, "We had to share the money between two charities." Use "Among" when discussing three or more of anything as in "The differences among the various tribes . . ." and "We divided the money among twenty charities."

Because and Since
Use the word "Since" to mean "after a specific time past." As an example, "Since I graduated, I have worked at several companies." Don't use "Since" to mean "for the reason that," as in "Since I graduated, I must have worked hard." It is confusing. Instead, use "Because I graduated, I must have worked hard."

Consul - Council - Counsel - Console
Let us examine five look-alike, sound-alike words whose meanings and pronunciations are not on the tip of everyone's tongue.

"Consul" comes from the Latin "consulere," to consult. In Roman times, a consul held the office of chief magistrate. At present, a consul is a government official (usually a member of the Foreign Service) residing abroad who represents some interests of the country of origin. Pronounce "Con" in "Consul" as you would pronounce the first three letters of "continental." Pronounce the "sul" part as you would pronounce the first four letters of "sully."

"Council" and "Counsel" have their origins in the same Latin word: "Concilium" (Com - together + calare - to call). In the Old French language (Middle Ages), we have "Cuncile," an assembly, and "Conseil," a consultation. "Council" and "Counsel" are pronounced alike. You may attempt to pronounce the last three letters of each word differently, but the result sounds stilted. "Coun" sounds just like "noun" and "town." The noun "council" has many meanings, too many to list here. American Indians held councils (pow-wows), and all over the U.S., city and county councils meet regularly. That should explain the meaning of "Council."

"Counsel" can be used as a noun, a transitive verb, and an intransitive verb. As a noun, it means "advice given," and it is used also as another word for "lawyer," particularly a lawyer in a court room. As a transitive verb, it means "to advise" as in the sentence "I counseled him to write a will." When used as an intransitive verb, it means "to consult" as in the sentence "I counseled with several agencies."

The fourth word, "console," is used occasionally, in error, as a substitute for one of the three words we have been discussing. A "console" is a desk-like structure that has knobs and meters all over it. When we visit NASA's mission control center in Houston by means of television, we are taken often to a room filled with consoles. Pronounce the first three letters of "console" as you pronounce the first three letters of "continental." Pronounce the last four letters of "console" as you pronounce the "sole" of a shoe. Use the word "console" when describing a box-like affair filled with electronic circuitry.

But wait a minute. "Console" is also a transitive verb meaning, "to comfort, to make less sad." In this usage, when pronouncing the word, place the emphasis in on the second syllable rather than on the first.

Each other - One another

Use "Each other" when discussing two people and "One another" when discussing three or more, as in the following sentences:

    A. Mary and Charles like each another.
    B. The members of the team seem to like one another.

Fewer and Less, Sufficient Number and Enough

Don't use "less" with a plural noun. For example, do not write "Less people . . ." or "We placed less orders . . ." Instead, use "fewer" with plural nouns: fewer people, fewer dollars, fewer grains of sand, fewer ears of corn. Use "less" only with commodities and other entities expressed with a singular noun: less money, less sand, less corn, less honesty.

Similarly, use "sufficient number" with plurals: a sufficient number of dollars. When the noun is not plural, use "enough": enough money.

Figuratively - Literally

People use "literally" occasionally as if it were a mere intensive, like "very" or "extremely." This is not only wrong but also almost the reverse of correct usage. "Literally" means "actually," "really," "factually." Use it in sentences in which the reader might otherwise believe that you're exaggerating or writing metaphorically. "Bill was literally white as a sheet He had covered his face with zinc oxide."

"Figuratively," on the other hand, assures your reader that you do not want your statement to be taken literally. In the following sentence, "kill" is figurative, a figure of speech: "Figuratively, I could kill you right now."

Going back to the first paragraph, if you just want to say that Bill was very pale and you didn't mind using clichés, you can write: "Bill was white as a sheet. He was scared to death." Note that this sentence doesn't use either "literally" or "figuratively." "Literally" would be incorrect and "figuratively" would be patronizing, like putting quotes around slang.

A possible explanation for the misuse of "literally": As its spelling suggests, it is related to the words "literature" and "letters." Hence, people may assume mistakenly that it means literary—rather than down-to-earth factual use of an expression. But in fact it says that the expression means exactly what the letters of the words say

Generation

Perhaps the time has come to restrict the use of the word "Generation" to the topic of genealogy. A father and mother and their children are one generation apart. A grandmother and grandfather are two generations apart from their grandchildren. When "Generation" is used to signify the passage of time, trouble brews, as in the phrase, " . . . the politics that have governed the U.S. for three generations." From the text that precedes the sentence above, we know that the writer is referring to life in our country from 1933 to the year 2000. How did the writer arrive at three generations? Did the writer divide sixty-seven years by three to arrive at twenty-two? Have we agreed that one generation covers twenty-two years? Do people reproduce that rapidly? The average over the centuries is three generations per century. Christ lived about 60 generations ago. Charlemagne (742-814) lived about 36 generations ago.

In discussing the policies that have governed the country since 1933, the writer can say, " . . . the policies that have governed the U.S. since the first inaugural of Franklin Roosevelt," or, " . . . the policies that have governed the U.S. since 1933."

People refer to the generation that fought World War II. The youngest person in the service was seventeen year old, or less. The oldest, perhaps a crusty admiral, was over sixty-five. Where is the generation? Why not refrain from identifying these people as a generation, and refer to them as "the Americans who fought in World Was II?"

Parameter and Perimeter

"Parameters" are the properties of a thing, real or unreal, living or not living, that determine its characteristics or behavior. Parameters used to determine the price of a racehorse, as an example, are age, weight, height, speed, track record, and blood line, among others. Parameters used to guess at the performance of the nation's economy next year would include interest rates, inflation rate, unemployment rate, levels of inventory, and corporate profits.

"Perimeter" is an outer boundary, say, the wall of a prison or the fence around a field. While the parameters of a concept, such as the nation's economy, have a perimeter, that is to say there is a finite number of parameters that describe the economy, one should not use these two words interchangeably. They are related only peripherally and the confusion stems from their sounding alike.

Quality

Writers and speakers think that when they use the word "quality," readers and listeners will know that they mean "high quality." Not so fast. Products of low quality are available from many sources. Products of medium quality are more prevalent than products of either high or low quality. Finally, products of high quality are the exception. They have high quality because they compare favorably to products of low and medium quality. In describing items that are the best that can be found in a category, these items should be described as having high quality, not simply as having quality.

Sanguine

Best not use the word "sanguine." The origin is from the French "sang," meaning "blood." So, "sanguine," the adjective, can mean "sanguinary" (bloodthirsty, murderous). But "sanguine" can also be used to describe a person with a reddish complexion, who, because of the color of the face, is thought to be healthy, confident, and optimistic. When one word can mean either "murderous" or "optimistic," the time has come to retire the word and rely on the words that convey the exact meaning, "murderous" and "optimistic."

Specious and Spurious

When losing ground in an argument, some think the best way to annihilate the opponent is to declare that his or her argument is either spurious or specious. The common perception is that using one or the other of these words indicates that you have superior knowledge that you will display in a moment, when you get the floor. Be wary of both words. "Spurious" comes from the Latin word "spurius" meaning false, or of illegitimate birth. Why tell your opponent that his or her argument is false, when in your heart of hearts, you wish to tell your opponent that he or she is an ignoramus? You may as well say that. It's more to the point. "Spurious" is not strong enough for the task at hand. It sounds impressive, but it may not convey your feelings.

If you tell your opponent that his or her argument is specious, you're in trouble. "Specious" comes from the Latin word "speciosus" meaning "beautiful" or "plausible." Over time, the meaning has changed to showy or having a false look of truth. You cannot demolish your opponent by saying that his or her argument is showy. If you want to indicate that your opponent is without a clue, you may as well get on with it.

"Specious" and "spurious" are fine words. The danger in using them in conversation is that there is no certainty anyone in the room knows the meaning the speaker intends to convey.

Talent

A talent is a special aptitude held by an individual such as an aptitude for mathematics or music; " . . . having talents in science," one might say. A talent is not the individual, it describes the individual, and saying, " . . . he distinguished himself as a talent in his own right . . ." is an inappropriate use of the word.

That, Which, and Who

In most cases, it is clear whether one uses "that," "which," or "who." Everybody says, "I do not know which fork to use," and no one says, "I do not know that fork to use." Confusion comes in sentences such as these:

> The buildings ---------are situated on the hill . . . .
> My mother's house --- is situated on the hill . . . .
> The people-------------swim in the ocean . . . .
> The cows---------------gave birth to these calves . . . .

We're dealing here with a cluster of problems: (1) Do we use "that" or "which"? (2) Do we use "that" or "who"? (3) Do we use "who" or "whom"?

In "The buildings ------ are situated on the hill," either "that" or "which" is correct. But in "My mother's house, <u>which</u> is situated on the hill, . . . , " and "My mother's house, <u>that</u> is situated on the hill, . . . , " the latter sounds clumsy. So don't use "that" after the comma. (The rule is that you don't use "that" to begin a non-restrictive clause. A non-restrictive clause is one that does not impart essential meaning to the sentence, as in "The gray horse, which I sold last year, had the longest tail I ever saw." A restrictive clause is one which cannot be omitted without changing the meaning of the sentence. The sentence "A roof that leaks needs repair" contains the restrictive clause "that leaks." If it were omitted, the meaning of the sentence would change.)

When do we write "who" rather that "that" or "which"? We have been taught to use "who" with humans, but this opens up the can of worms called "whom." The old word "whom" was in use every day a few years back. No longer. We used to ask, "To whom are you sending that package?" And, "I wish I knew to whom I should address these remarks." We felt good about ourselves when accomplishing the feat of using "whom" correctly. Those of us who remember the big bands and balanced federal budgets still use "whom" when indicated, and good for us. But nothing lasts forever. Even people who know grammar and syntax are abandoning "whom." Now for the grammar. "Who" is the subject of verbs, as in "Who will take a walk with me?" "Whom" is the object of verbs, as in "The interesting people whom I met read a great deal." ("Whom" is the object of "met.") "Whom" is also the object of prepositions, as in "The people to whom I sent

Christmas cards live on the west coast." ("Whom" is the object of the preposition "to.")

To those who are on the verge of quitting the field, do your best to hang on. "Whom" may return. If you write "A fireman who I met last week at the party . . ." and you're uneasy with writing "who" in place of the grammatically-correct "whom," try substituting "that," as in "A fireman <u>that</u> I met last week at the party . . ." (The title of one of Mark Twain's stories is "The Man <u>That</u> Corrupted Hadleysburg.")

Whether - If
When two choices are to be discussed as in the two sentences below, use "whether" rather than "if."

    A. I do not recall <u>whether</u> the room is blue or green. (not <u>if</u>)

    B. It makes no difference <u>whether</u> we do it today or tomorrow. (not <u>if</u>)

We hear speakers on occasion using "if" in sentences such as those above. But in writing, the usage is ambiguous. "Whether" is a clear indication that a fork in the road has been reached and that two choices are about to be explained. Not so with "if," which can also introduce the conditional or subjunctive moods, so that the reader must decide which "if" you mean. Play it safe and stick with "whether" in these choice-between-two-things sentences.

MISPRONOUNCED WORDS

Here are several words that are mispronounced frequently. The incorrect spelling of the words in capital letters represents the mispronunciation. The correct spelling follows in parentheses.

Asterik (Asterisk)
> Say "asteriSk." Don't leave out the S in front of the K.

Athalete (Athlete)
> Pronounce with two syllables only: "ath-lete," and leave out that second, imaginary A.

Auxilary (Auxiliary)
> Do not forget the second I. Some dictionaries allow dropping the second I, but leave it in if you can.

Awready (Already)
> Say "aLready."

Febuary (February)
> Slow down and make certain the sound "brew" is in the middle of the word.

Canadate (Candidate)
> The first D must be pronounced.

Congradjulations (Congratulations)
> Remove the DJ sound and insert CH, or be brave and pronounce the word as it is written, pronouncing the first T as T, and not as DJ.

Cuz (Because)

>We all say "cuz" in rapid-fire, informal conversation, but formal usage requires two syllables as in "be-cause." A few purists never say CUZ. Bless them.

Deteriate (Deteriorate)

>The standard pronunciation requires five syllables: "de-tir-e-AH-rate"—a mouthful.

Distrik (District)

>The pronunciation includes the final T̲.

Eggzit (Exit)

>If you can say ex-boyfriend, you can say EXIT.

Ekcetera (Etcetera)

>Pronounce the first T as T instead of K. The derivation is Latin: e̲t̲ (and) plus c̲e̲t̲e̲r̲a̲ (others).

Fer (For)

>Fer heavens sake, say FOR.

Ferget (Forget)

>See above. Say FORGET.

Fortay (Forte)

>If you use the word to mean someone's strong point, then the preferred pronunciation is FORT.

Gonna (Going) Say GOING, or once in a while say WILL.

Heighth (Height)

>There is no TH sound at the end of this word. This word sounds like MIGHT. We are in trouble when architects talk about the heig̲h̲t̲h̲ of buildings.

Hunert (Hundred)

>"Hun-Dred" is standard.

Lenth (Length)
>   Say LENGTH. Do not forget the G.

Libary (Library)
>   On rare occasions the R is left out.

Lugjury (Luxury)
>   The X in LUXURY is pronounced KSH so the word is pronounced LUCK-SHURY. (TV ads for fancy cars, ahem).

Muricun (American)
>   Say AMERICAN as in American flag. We must stop talking about the MURICAN flag, the MURICAN dream, and the great MURICAN people.

Ninedy (Ninety)
>   Say NINETY. Use a T in place of a D. (New Yorkers, beware). Everybody says NINETEEN correctly. We should be able to say NINETY.

Nuculer (Nuclear)
>   NU-CLE-AR, and not NU-CU-LER. (Secretaries of Defense and commanders of nuclear subs please take note).

Paticuly (Particularly)
>   Take your time. Say all five syllables, please.

Pennsavania (Pennsylvania)
>   Be certain to pronounce the L in Pennsylvania, William Penn's woods, one of the thirteen original states.

Periphial (Peripheral)
>   Say PERIPHERAL. Do not forget the R sound.

Pitshure (Picture)
>   Unless it contains liquid, pronounce the C as K.

Realator (Realtor)

> Please, it's REAL-TOR. Out with the second A.

Reconize (Recognize)

> Say it slowly and say it all. Add the G.

Silicon and **Silicone** (The spelling of these two words is correct.)

> The last two letters of SILICON are pronounced UN as in UNhand that maiden or UNtie your shoe. When referring to the area south of San Francisco, say SILICON VALLEY and pronounce it SILICUN VALLEY. Silicon is the element used in the manufacture of semiconductors. The material used for breast implants is SILICONE and the last three letters are pronounced OWN. SILICAHN does not exist.

Strenth (Strength)

> Say STRENGTH. Don't forget the G.

Subsiderary (Subsidiary)

> Say SUBSIDIARY. Out with that extra R.

Tempature (Temperature)

> It may be convenient to drop one of the syllables but say all five.

Wanna (Want to)

> See GONNA

We end this section with suggestions concerning two groups of words, some words that start with "H," and some words that have but one "L."

The "H" words. Most words that start with "H" are pronounced with a slight breathing-out sound at the beginning. This is the process of aspiration. So words such as "huge," "human," "hungry," and "Houston" are pronounced so that the listener hears the "H" sound at the front end. It is not correct to pronounce these words to sound like "uge," "uman," "ungry," and "Uston."

The "L" words. Most words that contain one "L" are pronounced with the "L" sound. The mistake is to change the "L" sound to a "Y" sound. Words that get this treatment on occasion are "civilian" and "Italian." This error in pronunciation could come from the permitted practice of pronouncing the double "L" as "Y" in some words such as "million" and "billion." In these two examples, the speaker has a choice of pronouncing the double "L" as "L" or "Y."

MISSPELLED WORDS

A few educated people misspell two words, "accommodate" and "supersede." And occasionally there is some confusion over these three word-pairs: "capital - capitol," "principal - principle," and "stationary - stationery."

Accommodate (correct spelling)
That second M is left out often. Reason? Perhaps we make an association with "Accumulate" which has one M.

Supersede (correct spelling)
When "Intercede," "Precede," and "Proceed" are spelled with a C, why use an S in the same location in the word "Supersede"? Let's look at the Latin derivations.

Intercede --- <u>inter</u> (between) and <u>cedere</u> (to go)
Precede ----- <u>pre</u> (before) and <u>cedere</u> (to go)
Proceed ----- <u>pro</u> (forward) and <u>cedere</u> (to go)
Supersede--- <u>super</u> (above) and <u>sedere</u> (to sit)

So there you have it. The first three have to do with some form of "to go" while the fourth has to do with "to sit." "Supersede" has two <u>s</u>'s. Confusion can be avoided by using "Replace."

Capital - Capitol
Use "capital" when referring to money, the top of a column, the death penalty, as in capital punishment, and the city that is the seat of government. Origin: Latin "capitalis," "of the head." Use "capitol" when referring to a building that houses government. Why? In Latin, the word "Capitolium" referred to the chief temple, the temple of Jupiter. It stood on the Capitoline Hill, the smallest of the seven hills of Rome. Washington, D.C., is the

nation's capital. The building where senators and members of the House of Representatives meet is the Capitol.

Principal - Principle

"Principal" used as an adjective means "the main item." As a noun it means "the person in charge." A "principle" means "a fundamental doctrine." Again from the Latin: there is an adjective "principalis," meaning "most important," and a noun "principium," meaning "the beginning." At some time, the <u>ple</u> ending was invented for "principium." (Try this for a mnemonic: Disci<u>ples</u> have princi<u>ples</u>.)

Stationary - Stationery

"Stationary" means motionless. "Stationery" refers to writing-paper for correspondence. The word comes from "stationer," a person who sells stationery. In the old days, such a person also sold books.

NEWSPEAK WORDS

Familiar words used in a different context and familiar words used in new combinations give us old words with new meanings. Some of them make us smile. We accept them. Others make us scratch our head because we fail to catch the meaning intended. The words are imprecise. When tempted to use one of the words we have listed below, or any one of hundreds of others, we should ask ourselves if their meanings will be transmitted exactly to their audience. If the meaning of the new word is too vague, give up on it and stick with the old word whose meaning is clear to everyone.

Let us start with a combination that brings a smile. "He went into the auto show room and came out with STICKER SHOCK." The phrase creates an amusing image. Hard to knock it, that is to say, er, it is difficult not to appreciate the amusing quality of the combination of the words sticker and shock.

We continue with the imprecise words that make us ponder as we search for the exact meaning intended by the user of these words.

Bottom Line.
Accountants will tell you that the bottom line of the Profit and Loss statement is after-tax earnings or after-tax earnings-per-share. The bottom line owes its importance to the eagerness with which financial analysts scan annual reports to find this number before they read any other data. BOTTOM LINE now means any important result such as bringing peace, ending famine, batting 0.400, and winning a tennis match. It also signifies a person who is attentive to the bottom line. "He is really a BOTTOM-LINE guy." Our recommendation is to restrict the use of BOTTOM LINE to its meaning in accounting. As for the BOTTOM-LINE guy, say he is effective.

Payoff.

This word once had an illegal overtone. On occasion, judges, elected officials and other individuals with power did someone a favor and after the fact the recipient of the favor paid off. The payoff could be a smoked ham, a couple tickets to a ball game, or better yet, a briefcase containing a half-million dollars in unmarked bills. The meaning of PAYOFF has changed. PAYOFF does not now always signify a shady deal. PAYOFF can be synonymous with <u>results</u>. It can be used in place of BOTTOM LINE when dramatic impact is not required. "I subscribed to the <u>Economist</u> the other day. I expect a big PAYOFF." Stick with <u>results</u>. Better image.

Rollout.

When the Boeing Company rolled the first 747 out of the hangar onto the field, an imaginative person, perhaps a press agent, described the event as a ROLLOUT. That event appears to be the origin of the term. ROLLOUT is now being used in conjunction with movies, plays, novels, shoes, and the latest fashions in the rag trade. In the old days, we said <u>introduced</u>, but this poor word is in temporary eclipse, replaced on most occasions by <u>debuted</u>, <u>premiered</u> and our friend here, ROLLED-OUT. "ABC Cola said it would introduce SweetWater in 10 cities early next year, as a prelude to a national ROLLOUT within six months." Save ROLLOUT for activity around hangars and use <u>promotion</u>, or <u>advertising campaign</u> instead.

Downsized.

The foreign competition and changing tastes among buyers suggested to American car manufacturers that they produce cars smaller than the standard products of the 1970s. This process of reducing length, weight and horsepower of cars was called DOWNSIZING. Now the term is applied to the acts of eliminating many positions in middle management, increasing productivity, and cutting costs in any way that comes to mind. There is lack of precision here. Manufacturing a car smaller than the collector's items from the '70s can be termed DOWNSIZING, but making changes in the structure of management and increasing the level of automation should not be called DOWNSIZING. These business activities should be identified for what they are. We want precision.

Hands-on.

Early in the introduction of computers into the office, people had to be trained in their use. One could not read about computers and expect to learn how to use them. Anyone who read the instruction manuals and hoped to learn about the use of computers went away mad (crazy). The only technique that was found to be successful in teaching novice computer-users to be proficient was to sit them in front of a computer and make them learn the techniques that they would use in their work. That process was called HANDS-ON training. Hands on the computer.

President Clinton held a meeting of business people in Arkansas. After the meeting, one interested party observed, "I hope that the president remains a HANDS-ON person." When terms such as HANDS-ON mean anything to somebody, they mean nothing to anybody. Save HANDS-ON for training requiring interaction with machinery. As for the interested party commenting on President Clinton, he could have said that he hoped the president would remain <u>involved</u> or <u>concerned</u>.

Upscale.

"It's still good, but it's not that incredible upscale service." The waiters no longer wear tuxedos? The chauffeured limousines are gone? UPSCALE, what mean? The dictionary tell us it means <u>stylish</u>. But it would be helpful to know precisely how the service has deteriorated. Details please, not one-word summaries whose meaning cannot be pinned down.

World-class.

"Imagine, for a moment, the panic that would hit any other world-class financial center . . ." We ask, what constitutes a WORLD-CLASS financial center? Number of skyscrapers, shares traded per day at the stock exchange, number of blue suits worn? Bye-bye WORLD-CLASS. Say "important."

If one must use the expression, it is safe to do so here: "Carl Lewis is a WORLD-CLASS runner because he wins track events against the best in the world."

Fine-tune.

Does anyone remember the early radios which had three tuning knobs rather than one? Those were the days before some genius invented in the 1920s the super-heterodyne receivers whose circuitry is part of today's radios. Before the invention, one had to know three dial settings to tune in a particular radio station. That was FINE TUNING. Financial writers now use the term FINE-TUNING. These writers tell us that FINE-TUNING describes the activities of elected officials who attempt to change Gross Domestic Product by adjusting interest rates, tariff barriers, tax rates, and the magnitude of the deficit. Please do not say FINE-TUNING, tell us in detail about the actions of these elected officials. Indeed, FINE-TUNING means adjusting a device or a system for maximum effectiveness, but when discussing the economy writers should know that we readers are interested in the intricate details.

Back Burner.

There were restaurants in France, there may still be some, that kept a soup going for as long as a week. As the patrons ordered some of the soup and reduced the level in the pot, the chef would add new ingredients and push the pot to the back of the stove, the coolest part, where the soup would simmer and be served the next day. This style of making soup gave birth to the phrase, "put it on the back-burner." Of course, the wood—and coal-burning stoves in those old restaurants had no burners, just a spot on the rear of the stove that was cooler than the front, or business, part. BACK-BURNER is the translation into English for that spot on the rear of the stove. When a commentator on reading habits says, "Classic literature had been put on the back burner over time," we are not certain whether old books are stacked on the rear of the stove, or new literature is added as the old is taken down by clients to be read. What is taking place? Writers need to be precise.

Quantum Leap or Quantum Jump.

A quantum is both a discrete amount of energy and a very small amount of energy. Try to imagine the amount of energy required to alter the orbit of one electron rotating around one proton (the model of the hydrogen atom). It is a very small amount of energy, but it is a discrete amount for each electron of each element. The concept behind the word QUANTUM is that the amount being discussed is discrete and predictable, not that the amount is either small or large. Writers who say "Third World countries are experiencing quantum increases in their usage of energy" should say instead that the rate of usage will increase by so many megawatts per year and then relate that number of megawatts to the number of megawatts consumed each year in Pittsburgh. We need accuracy. Perhaps writers who use "quantum increases" mean "order of magnitude" increases, which latter expression means "ten times larger." Our sample sentence, then, would read "Third World countries are experiencing order-of-magnitude increases in their usage of energy."

Radar Screen.

The word <u>radar</u> is a contraction of <u>r</u>adio <u>d</u>etecting <u>a</u>nd <u>r</u>anging. A radio beam is emitted from an electronic system and if a portion is reflected by an object, say an airplane, then some characteristics of the object causing the reflection can be determined, such as its distance from the system, its size, direction, and velocity. Writers and broadcasters have picked up the phrase <u>radar screen</u> and we read and hear that "Slashing Medicare has dropped off the radar screen of most members of Congress" and that " . . . . the next country to suffer financial chaos is about to appear on the radar screen." Readers and listeners would like to have the data on the radar screen interpreted and accounted for. It is not informative enough to tell us that various topics are popping on and off somebody's screen.

Cutting Edge.

Apparently people in all professions can do cutting-edge work. One reads that artists, heart surgeons, musicians, physicists, and people who manufacture those electronic miracles, microprocessors, all live at the cutting edge. Swords have cutting edges. Double-edged swords must have two cutting edges. The common razor has a cutting edge. Pathologists take thin slices of organs and examine them under microscopes. Pathologists must have cutting edges in order to take thin slices. Do artists at the cutting edge have paint brushes that the rest of us have not heard about? Do musicians at the cutting edge play without instruments? I think we are on to NEWSPEAK. Sounds good, means little.

Real World.

According to some writers, our world, our planet, has a section called the real world. Although it is not stated, the implication is that the remainder of the planet is made up of the unreal world. Judging from the context in which the term "real world" is found, "real world" people are industrialists who meet payrolls, people who work with their hands, and people who work up a sweat. Those whose experiences in life do not permit them to be considered "real world" people work in universities, isolated in their ivory towers, toil on newspapers, writing and editing the daily output, administer think tanks, write poetry, and study pre-Islamic Arabic. Let it be said here that there is no unreal world. All worlds, all people, all occupations are real. They may not be the same, but they are real. No more REAL WORLD, please.

Soft Landing.

The space program of the United States differs from that of the former Soviet Union in many respects including re-entry to the Earth from space of astronauts and cosmonauts. Astronauts' vehicles dangle from parachutes and land in the ocean, a soft landing, while cosmonauts' vehicles dangle from parachutes and land in Siberia, a hard landing. Economists, in need of an expression to describe their wishes for the American economy in the near term, adopted SOFT LANDING. It is supposed by economists, and perhaps by politicians as well, that readers will understand that SOFT LANDING means unemployment will increase 1.2%, the prime rate will go up to 7%, and inflation will stay under control as taxes are increased in order to balance the budget in seven years. Well, dream on. Readers understand landings in the ocean versus landings of the hard turf of Siberia, but not the relationship between these landings and economic forecasts. Economists, politicians, and reporters who write on matters effecting the economy need to tell us in detail the cause and effect of various steps put in place by the Federal Reserve, the Congress, and the Administration, which are intended to restore us to prosperity. No shorthand, please.

Get a Handle on.
Some writers refuse to use that old standby, <u>understand</u>. They say instead, that people are GETTING A HANDLE ON a problem or an issue. One has images of a problem or an issue being taken to the workshop in the basement where handles are screwed on. While adding handles increases portability, it adds nothing to understanding. People either do or do not understand a problem or an issue. There is no need to add handles. A thorough study of the problem or issue is called for and perhaps because a thorough study is much harder work than attaching handles, attaching handles gets the nod. Spare us, please.

Fair Share.
During the 1992 presidential campaign, Governor Clinton castigated rich taxpayers for not having paid taxes in sufficient amount. He claimed that they had not paid their fair share and ought to be ashamed for their laxity. The flailing of the rich resumed during 1993 as President Clinton reminded the rich once again that they had not been paying their fair share of taxes. There must be magic in using the term fair share without defining its meaning—the Congress obliged the president by passing a tax measure that raised the tax rates on large incomes. It appears that while 31% did not qualify as a fair share in 1992, 39.6% did in 1993 and presently.

The undefined fair share has now branched out beyond taxation to include the publication of federal regulations as in this sentence: "The Food and Drug Administration has added more that its fair share of regulations." By implication, we divide the number of regulations placed on the books per year by the number of federal agencies entitled to author regulations, and any agency publishing more than that quotient has acted unfairly toward the American people. Would writers spare us the concept of fair share—get rid of fairness as a measure of taxation or numbers of regulations, or anything else, for that matter?

Memorialize.

When we wish to commemorate an event or a person, we are free to declare a national holiday or construct another memorial in Washington, D.C. The word "memorialize" is associated with the word "commemorate." Let us use "memorialize" in that sense. In the last few years, writers and speakers have been associating "memorialize" with the process of placing a memo (memorandum) in a filing cabinet. These writers and speakers are doing the verbal equivalent of carving into stone the contents of a memo. They ought to cease and desist from this practice. Here is a sentence that demonstrates this improper use. "They talked at length with angry constituents and memorialized the information in internal correspondence." The old fashioned way of expressing the same thought is: "They talked at length with angry constituents, took detailed notes, and placed these notes in their files."

Window of Opportunity.

The introduction of computers required new words and old words with new meanings to describe human actions and electronic activity. Software, modem, input, terminal, and window are a few words that come to mind. The word "window," in computer talk signifies a moment when an operator may do something before the program moves to the next step. "Window of opportunity" grew out of "window" as in this sentence, "The passage of this bill gives Congress a 45-day window of opportunity to prevent the implementation of programs." By changing "day" from singular to plural, we can eliminate "window of opportunity" as in this rewrite: "The passage of this bill gives Congress 45 days to prevent the implementation of programs." "Window of opportunity" is a long-winded NEWSPEAK word that serves no purpose.

*   *   *   *

The disadvantage of using NEWSPEAK words and combinations of words is that the listener or reader may not know the meaning that the speaker or writer intends. One can read, as an example, that such-and-such company manufactures 2100 pharmaceutical products in plants located in seven countries, has 17,000 employees and sales of five billion dollars per year, or one can read that such-and-such company is WORLD-CLASS. Which is more precise? The suspicion does arise that users of NEWSPEAK welcome the imprecision of these terms. After all, is it not easier to say that a certain company is WORLD-CLASS than to do the research required to authenticate the opinion?

NON-EXISTENT WORDS

Heighth

The word is "Height" and it rhymes with "Might." Many people add an H to "Height" and change the final sound from T to Th. Even architects fall into this trap. (Those architects who say "The heighth of this building is . . ." did not make it to class that day). Why would people add a letter and change the final sound of this word? Here is an explanation: "Width," "Depth," "Breadth" and "Length" deal with measurements and therefore are companions of "Height," so why not pronounce all endings the same way? Because it's wrong, that's why not.

Irregardless

"Irregardless" may be a mistaken combination of "Irrespective" and "Regardless." In any event, it does not exist. "Regardless" is standard.

Orientated

Say "He was oriented by his new instructor," instead of "He was orientated by his new instructor." The shorter form is more efficient. Our British cousins say "orientated," but they speak a different brand of English.

NOUNS AS ADJECTIVES

In speaking and writing English, we often use nouns as adjectives. There are two-noun combinations such as "dog house," and three-noun combinations such as "income tax payments." In the first example, "dog" is the noun acting as an adjective, modifying "house," and in the second example, "income tax" consists of two nouns acting together as an adjective to modify "payments." These combinations serve the purpose of shortening sentences by removing prepositions. "Dog house" is a contraction of "house of the dog." "Income tax payments" is a contraction of "payments of taxes on income." As long as these contractions do not cause confusion, they are acceptable and useful. The meanings of two-noun and of most three-noun combinations are clear, but users should know that combinations of several nouns can be misunderstood. Unless the combination is clear, writers and speakers will do well to break up the series of nouns by saying "payments of income taxes" in place of "income tax payments." Here are some combinations heard frequently.

Two Nouns	Three Nouns
litmus test	ice cream sundae
state television	record budget deficits
return evaluations	paper doll tax
problem banks	prestige private school
sentence structure	gate-keeper physicians
top earner	executive branch authority

Here is an example of a three-noun combination whose meaning may not be clear at first reading:

"She conducted a <u>cost benefit analysis</u> on the insurance policy."

Do we mean an analysis of the costs of various benefits, or the analysis of the benefits of various costs? As there are no benefits to costs, the sentence must mean an analysis of benefits. Here is a version without ambiguity:

"She conducted an analysis of costs versus benefits of each feature of the insurance policy." We have a few more words, but we have clarity as well.

Here are three four-noun combinations that might convey the intended meanings if they were broken up as indicated inside the parentheses. Four-noun combinations are not always clear.

A. Disability income risk exposures (Exposures to the risk of not receiving disability income)

B. Bomb damage assessment pictures (Pictures providing the assessment of bomb damage)

C. Fire control management regulations (Regulations for managing fire control procedures) or perhaps (Promulgation from management of fire control procedures)

Speaking of nouns that act as adjectives, the word "Fun" has been forced into double duty for the last decade. It is a well-respected noun, as in the sentence "I had <u>fun</u> at your party." But some speakers are casting it in the role of an adjective, as in the sentence "I worked on selecting routes for the interstate highway system. It was a <u>fun</u> project." Say "amusing," "exciting," or "interesting" instead of <u>fun</u> when the sentence calls for an adjective.

PHYSICAL DIMENSIONS

Words in the English language that are used to describe lengths, shapes, and locations, such as <u>deep</u>, <u>broad</u>, <u>solid</u>, and <u>area</u>, have gained other meanings. Sentences are given below to illustrate the point. In each case, the sentence is re-written in parentheses using a more precise word than the dimensional (underlined) word used in the quote.

"She is a <u>deep</u>-thinker." (She thinks clearly.)

"These are assets taken from lenders in <u>deep</u> trouble." (These are assets taken from lenders with insufficient funds.)

"Government bonds were assigned a risk-weighing factor of zero." (Government bonds were promoted as investments without risk.)

"It is important to embrace far-reaching technologies." (It is important to invest in the technologies that will have applications in the next century.)

"If there is a tax vacuum, it will be filled." (If there exist goods and services not taxed, governments will learn to tax them.)

"He must pick a <u>solid</u> team of cabinet members." (He must select a team of qualified cabinet members.)

"This department is blessed with several top researchers." (This department is blessed with several eminent researchers.)

"Would you happen to know her <u>areas</u> of responsibility?" (Would you happen to know her responsibilities?)

"We are being overwhelmed by the <u>volume</u> (or <u>mass</u>) of data." (We are being overwhelmed by the amount of data.)

"We need a <u>view</u> of the tax and cost structure." (We need to understand taxes and costs.)

"The broad public approves of what Governor Jones is doing." (The majority of the public approves of Governor Jones' administration.)

Concerning unwanted animals in the United States: "Nationwide, the total is in the area of 15 to 20 million." (There are between 15 and 20 million unwanted animals in the United States.)

"But where the British system is based on the fusion of powers, ours is based on the separation of powers." (Whereas the British system is based on the fusion of powers, ours is based on the separation of powers.)

"Because it is extremely hard to rebuild a country from head to toe using only internally-generated funds . . ." (Because it is difficult to rebuild a country completely using only internally-generated funds . . .)

We are left with a wide range of options. (We are left with many options).

POPULAR WORDS

Some words come into use because they are catchy, or because they serve the purposes of writers of advertising copy, or because they add to one's perception of an object a desirable quality which does not exist, or for other reasons unknown. These words, and combinations of words, are with us a while, and like slow comets, they disappear. Using these words does not constitute errors in syntax, just a departure from standard English. Note that in a previous section, NEWSPEAK, we identified words and word combinations which lack precision and leave the reader in search of intended meaning. The words listed here do not lack precision particularly. They are objected to because they have "caught on" in popular writing and are over-used and therefore tiresome. Over-used words can drive you bats. Here are some examples of words that arrived a while ago and are fading, some that are still with us currently, and others that have just made their appearance.

Eminence grise (Fading)
A few years ago, one could not pick up a weekly news magazine without reading that yet another important person was named an <u>eminence grise</u>. If the writer had identified the person as someone who worked behind the scenes, or as someone who was the power behind the throne, we would have understood the position right away. We have the dictionary to thank for shining light into this dark corner. A certain Catholic priest, Francois du Tremblay, a monk and diplomat, was an assistant to Cardinal Richelieu (1585-1642), the chief minister of Louis XIII. The priest wore grey vestments, and the cardinal wore red. Because cardinals are addressed as eminences, it happened that our priest was given the nick-name <u>eminence grise</u> and the cardinal <u>eminence rouge</u>.

Myriad (Appeared recently)

Myriad is the Greek word for ten thousand. As an adjective it means <u>countless</u>. As a noun, it means a <u>great number</u>. Writers are injecting this word into sentences in place of the word <u>many</u>. On close examination of the sentences that carry the word <u>myriad</u>, it appears that the writers thought they could get away with indicating some number larger than three by saying <u>myriad</u>. After seeing the word a few times, readers start to thirst for precision. How many, did you say? Not ten thousand, certainly.

Gourmet (Has been around a while and is still in use)

The French noun <u>gourmet</u> is used whenever possible by people who sell anything from coffee to pots and pans. We have <u>gourmet</u> kitchens, <u>gourmet</u> sections in the supermarkets, <u>gourmet</u> restaurants, and <u>gourmet</u> ice cream. This decent, law-abiding French noun has become an over-used American adjective. A <u>gourmet</u> is a connoisseur of good food and wines. You could find a <u>gourmet</u> at a fine restaurant once a week enjoying a special meal served with the appropriate wines. If there is an opposite to a <u>gourmet</u>, is it a <u>gourmand</u>, a glutton. How did we survive as a country before we started identifying so many items and experiences as <u>gourmet</u>?

Real Pro (In current use)

As we all know, a professional sports figure accepts money for services. The expression "<u>real</u> pros" suggests that some people possess talents that mere pros do not have. Their additional talents are too difficult to identify, and therefore are not enumerated. Writers who use the expression might tell us that "<u>real</u> pros" are outstanding athletes and be done with it. No code, please.

Boutique (In current use)

Boutiques are shops that sell certain types of merchandise such as leather goods, linens, and pottery. We read now about <u>boutique</u> law firms. What does that mean? Law firms do indeed specialize. Some practice family law, others handle bankruptcies, still others haggle with the IRS over taxes, and yet others assist their corporate clients. Is a <u>boutique</u> law firm one that practices an arcane specialty within the broad specialty? The questionable use of <u>boutique</u> is not limited to law firms. A reporter writes this lead for an article on solar power: "Dismissed for two decades as a <u>boutique</u> power source best used for fringe electricity users . . . ." Are we to gather that solar power is used to illuminate small stores selling specialities?

Foreign words should be added to the English language (taco, diktat, coup d'état) when there is no handy substitute. Foreign words that confuse us (<u>boutique</u> as applied to law firms and solar power) should be left in their countries of origin.

REDUNDANCIES

Here are examples of the use of more words than are necessary to convey the thought. In the examples below, the words written in the upper case need not be there. They are redundant.

TRUE facts   I PERSONALLY feel
VERY fundamental   PARTICULARLY wrong
ABSOLUTE certainty   TOTALLY obsolete
BRIEF summary   I JUST want to thank you.

And these redundant bloopers:

I think it could POSSIBLY change.

It will take a while for your eyes to adjust GRADUALLY to the light.

If you are a single person AND NOT MARRIED . . .

And these last four from sportscasters:

It's all up to the batter, FOR THE MOST PART.

Concerning a coach pacing the sideline: He must be MENTALLY thinking about . . .

Concerning a linesman handling the chains: I believe he's giving it a VISUAL look.

He's extremely versatile. HE CAN DO MANY THINGS.

The examples given above contain obviously redundant expressions. Here are samples of subtle redundancies, but redundancies nonetheless.

"The Nicene Creed was written originally in 325." (It was written once, not several times, so no need to say originally.)

"The Stock market drifted aimlessly." (Drifting is always aimless.)

"We must see a collaboration between business and government, a joint effort to develop programs that will benefit industry." (If business and government are working together, no need to use joint.) (Try: "We must have a collaborative effort between business and government to develop programs that will benefit industry.")

A comment concerning the forests of the North West brings us this double redundancy: "Of course, we do an annual harvest every year, but we are not guilty of wholesale decimation." (No comment required on the appearance, side by side, of annual and every year. Decimation means to destroy a large part of something such as an army or a forest. No need to say wholesale.)

"The rules require banks to evaluate consumer loans effective as of March 31, 1992." (Use either effective or as of, not both.)

"It has a dozen interior features arranged on the console so that you can find what you need while operating the car at the same time." (Bye, bye at the same time.)

"The results are partially traceable to the cumulative impact of the value-added tax over many years." (Cumulative and over many years say the same thing. Take your pick. Use one only.)

" . . . use it to say over and over again . . ." (. . . use it to say over and over, or . . . use it to say again and again . . .)

In the remaining examples, it is not necessary to add a comment to identify the redundant element. Underlining by the reader does the job.

Moving expenses of a married couple can be claimed if either separately meets the distance and work requirements.

The two both failed to use the experience learned at work.

Previous elections over the past thirty years

We must prepare for the future that lies ahead of us.

The concepts merged together.

Three different ways

Each individual person

They worked together collectively.

The events were reported by two different newspapers on two different occasions.

Co-exist together

My own personality

Very first

The single greatest challenge

We want to predict future events

True original

Each and every year

Key importance

Unvarnished truth

Apparent fact

Standard cliché

Basic principle

Added bonus

Variety of different reasons

Future generations yet to come

WEST COAST WORDS

Sierra Nevada
"Sierra" is the Spanish word for mountain range. "Nevada" is the Spanish word for snow-covered. The Sierra Nevada is the snow-covered mountain range that runs along the eastern border of California. The most common expression used when discussing this mountain range is "The Sierra," and that is correct. Some writers and conversationalists use the expression, "The Sierras." Because there is only one mountain range in that part of the country, the plural cannot be correct. Stick with "The Sierra."

Once in a while, one sees in print, "the Sierra Nevada mountain range." That's redundant with a capital R.

"Sierra" and "Sierra Nevada" are correct. It is surprising how many Californians say "The Sierras." Of all people, they should know the source of their drinking water.

Cities
This entry could have been placed under mispronounced words. BOISE, the capital of Idaho, is pronounced with a soft S; sounds like BOY SEA. HELENA, the capital of Montana, is pronounced HELEN as in the woman's name, followed by A as in the second A in TACOMA. SPOKANE is pronounced SPOKE followed by the woman's name ANNE. Natives and locals of these cities are certain to correct those who mispronounce the name of their hometown. They are at their worst when doing so.

California

While discussing place names of the west, we take the opportunity of pointing out the obvious, that California is not the largest state, as many reporters write. Alaska is the largest state. California is the most populous state in the nation, a dubious distinction.

MISCELLANEOUS STUFF

AFFECT AND EFFECT
BASICALLY
e.g. AND i.e.
THE FACT THAT
FOR FREE
GENDER NEUTRALITY
HYPHENATING NUMBERS
I AND ME
ITS, IT'S, AND ITS'
-IZE, LIKE, AND -WISE
LATER, LATTER, AND LATEST
LATIN ABREVIATIONS
LIKE AND AS
NOT ONLY AND BUT ALSO
PERIOD AND TIME
PUNCTUATION
SEQUENCE
UNIQUE
WEEDS
WHAT

AFFECT AND EFFECT

The bad news about "affect" and "effect"—the reason they are difficult to use correctly—is that they pack four meanings into two spellings. Worse still, three of these meanings are related closely.

The good news is that only two meanings are common, and you can reduce these to a simple rule: the verb is spelled "affect," the noun is spelled "effect." Here are the four meanings, beginning with the two common ones:

1. This is a <u>verb</u> that means <u>to change or influence something</u>. It is spelled "affect," with an "A":

    How did your actions <u>affect</u> your brother?

    He realized that these experiences <u>affected</u> his ideas and had been <u>affecting</u> them for a long time.

2. This is a <u>noun</u> that means <u>the result of something</u>. It is spelled "effect," with an "E." It has a related adjective form spelled "effective":

    It's a simple case of cause and <u>effect</u>.

    What was the <u>effect</u> of these actions upon your brother?

    What's the most <u>effective</u> treatment?

3. This is a seldom-used verb that means <u>to bring something about, to cause some condition to exist</u>. It is spelled "effect," with an "E":

A few physicians have been able to <u>effect</u> a cure.

A new policy is beginning to <u>effect</u> change in the stock market.

4. This word—currently used only as a technical medical or psychological term—is a <u>noun</u> that means <u>an emotion, especially of attraction or repulsion</u>. It is spelled "affect," with an "A." It is related to the adjective "affective." These quotations are taken from technical ournals:

Their psychic lives are overfull of complexes, levels and <u>affects</u>.

Love and hate are <u>affective</u> phenomena.

BASICALLY

About thirty years ago, the word "basically" was upon us. It has become a crutch. Many Americans cannot open a paragraph without leaning heavily on "basically." The virus has spread, infecting English-speaking people worldwide. Television programs emanating from faraway places such as Pakistan show educated people saying "basically."

Mankind has managed to stamp out plagues and diseases. What can be done about "basically"? Could we stop using the word, and while we are at it, toss out those other crutches, "actually," "arguably," "essentially," and "hopefully" when they are used as fillers?

Here are examples of sentences containing fillers that read and sound better when the fillers are eliminated, or when alternative sentence structure is used as in the case of "hopefully":

"I actually saw him jump." (I saw him jump.)

"It is arguably the best tax plan." (It is the best tax plan.)

"Essentially, he has met all the requirements." (He has met all the requirements.)

"Hopefully, they will go on to win the pennant." (We hope that they will go on to win the pennant.)

For years authors have been modifying adjectives and verbs with the adverb "relatively." These authors do not complete the thought by telling us relative to what? An example: "There were relatively few people in the stands." That's all very well, but relative to which day, or to which event. "There were few people in the stands Saturday afternoon." That's better. "There were 5,000 people in the stands." That's best.

e.g. AND i.e.

The two abbreviations "e.g." and "i.e." have slightly different meanings. After reading "e.g.," the reader expects to be provided with one or more examples. After reading "i.e.," the reader expects to be told the complete concept, be it in one word or in a long list, or in a phrase.

"e.g." is the abbreviation for the Latin words "exempli gratia," meaning "free examples," and we use it to mean "for example." Read the following sentence out loud: "It happens frequently that creative people start out in one discipline but become known in another, for example, Somerset Maugham and the painter Ingres." Note that when saying "for example," there is a pause before and after the expression. When writing, one indicates the pauses with commas. (Maugham studied for a career in medicine. Ingres [1780-1867] played the violin as a child and was proficient enough to perform publicly. His father, a sculptor, determined that the boy would be a painter. Although the boy accommodated his father's wishes, he hid a violin under his bed and cranked away on it when his parents were out of the house. The expression "violin d'Ingres" still means "hobby" in French.)

"e.g." is not used in conversation, but the sentence above would read as follows if "e.g." were to replace "for example": "It happens frequently that creative people start out in one discipline but become known in another, e.g., Somerset Maugham and the painter Ingres."

"i.e." is the abbreviation for the Latin words "id est," meaning "that is." As above, set off "id est" with commas before and after. "i.e." can be thought of as an equal sign. The reader expects a restatement for purposes of clarification. Here is an example: "When cooking this dish, novices can use the two basic seasonings, i.e., salt and pepper." In most instances, a well-informed reader would know the information that follows "i.e." That is the case with salt and pepper, and it is also the case in this phrase: " . . . the City of Light, i.e., Paris."

The nonstandard varieties of these abbreviations have an amusing inventiveness:

-e.g.   -e.g.,   -e.g.-   e.g.,   e.g.,   eg.   e.g, (all incorrect)

THE FACT THAT

In our drive to eliminate needless words from sentences while saving the meaning, we can condense most sentences that contain the expressions <u>for the fact</u>, <u>due to the fact</u>, or <u>because of the fact</u>. Here are examples. The version with fewer words is placed in parentheses after the example.

1. I would be content to leave it at that, were it not for <u>the fact that</u> she is free to choose the car she prefers. (I would be content to leave it at that, were it not that she is free to choose the car she prefers.)

2. Angelica makes no secret of <u>the fact that</u> she was born Agnes Smith. (Angelica admits that she was born Agnes Smith.)

3. <u>By virtue of the fact that</u> militant Islam is the enemy of the Arab states that Israel is negotiating with, . . . (Because militant Islam is the enemy of the Arab states with which Israel is negotiating, . . .)

4. His past support for Communism can be explained <u>by virtue of the fact that</u> he was only 22 in 1937. (His past support for communism may be due to his being only 22 in 1937.)

5. The play is a collection of one-acts that are unrelated except <u>for the fact that</u> they all take place in the same hotel rooms. (The play is a collection of one-acts that are unrelated except that they take place in the same hotel rooms.)

FOR FREE

The adjective <u>free</u> is being used as a noun in this popular sentence: "I got these tickets for free." If we keep using adjectives as nouns, we might start saying "I go to Lake Tahoe for HAPPY" when we mean to say "I go to Lake Tahoe for happy times."

How to use <u>free</u>:
    The meals were free.
    The tickets were free.
    It was a free lunch!
    I received free tickets in the mail.

<u>Free</u> is an adjective. Use it to modify nouns. One says "Free tickets for the exhibit were available."

Do not forget the substitute <u>at no charge</u>. "The tickets for the exhibit at the museum were available at no charge."

GENDER NEUTRALITY

An aspect of the women's movement that we dare not overlook (and rightly so) is the use of <u>his</u> or <u>him</u> exclusively when we mean <u>hers</u> and <u>her</u> as well. In other words, we can no longer refer to the male as the typical human being. Because many writers find that using <u>his or her</u> is clumsy, we offer a way out. Here are two versions of a sentence. We say that if possible, avoid <u>his or her</u> and try <u>their</u>.

OK: Each member must pay his or her dues by May 1.
HOW ABOUT? All members must pay their dues by May 1.

<u>Their</u> is not to be overlooked as a way around the dilemma posed by the legitimate requirement that language be more neutral now than in the good old days when good old boys controlled it. Move the sentence from singular to plural as in this example:

"An important part of the analysis is learning the amount of the client's assets because it will determine his or her interest in buying."

Changing to the plural:

"An important part of the analysis is learning the amount of clients' assets because it will determine their interest in buying."

HYPHENATING NUMBERS

When we write a check from our personal checking account, we are asked to state the amount of the check in both digits and words. For example, we make out a check to the phone company in the amount of $87.32. When we write this amount in words, where shall we place the hyphens? Here is the rule: use hyphens in the numbers from twenty-one through ninety-nine, and nowhere else. How would you write this number in words: 217,328? Answer: two hundred seventeen thousand, three hundred twenty-eight. Note that only one hyphen is called for, and note further that one writes "two hundred seventeen thousand" and not "two hundred and seventeen thousand," and that one writes "three hundred twenty-eight," and not "three hundred and twenty-eight." The "and" crops up in conversation, as in "two hundred and seventeen thousand," but the "and" is not used in writing.

There is an exception. In compound-adjective phrases such as "pay-as-you-go financing" or "well-traveled road," you use hyphens to hold the adjective together. Hence you write "four-billion-year life of the planet," using a hyphen in a number even though the phrase does not include a number from twenty-one through ninety-nine.

I and ME

No one says "from I," "to I," or "for I." But millions say, "from Tom and I," "to Nancy and I," and "for Chuck and I."

After prepositions such as <u>against</u>, <u>for</u>, <u>to</u>, <u>between</u> and <u>after</u>, use the formal English <u>me</u> and not <u>I</u>. The existence of <u>and</u>, separating Tom, Nancy and Chuck from the rest of the sentence, does not eliminate the need to say <u>me</u>. So the phrases said or written correctly are <u>from Tom and me</u>, and <u>for Chuck and me</u>.

    Correct: From Tom and me
    Wrong: From Tom and I

    Correct: To Nancy and me
    Wrong: To Nancy and I

    Correct: For Chuck and me
    Wrong: For Chuck and I

    Correct: Just between you and me
    Wrong: Just between you and I

The same rule applies to <u>I</u> and <u>me</u> after verbs. Do not say "He sent Tom and I a gift" or "He drove Chuck and I to the store." Use a <u>me</u> in place of the <u>I</u>. Use the accusative case (<u>me</u>, <u>us</u>, <u>him</u>, <u>her</u>, <u>them</u>) when a pronoun is the object of a verb, except for the verb <u>to be</u>. (In English, we do not decline nouns and adjectives as is done in Latin, but we still decline pronouns.)

    Correct: He sent Tom and me a gift.
    Wrong: He sent Tom and I a gift.

    Correct: He drove Chuck and me to the store.
    Wrong: He drove Chuck and I to the store.

ITS, IT'S and ITS'

English spelling is neither fair nor logical. Its illogical features are rooted in its history—a tale too long to tell here. Take it on good authority, then, that:

<u>Its</u> is the possessive form of <u>it</u>: "Do not judge a book by its cover."

<u>It's</u> is the contraction of <u>it is</u> or <u>it has</u>: "It's raining. It's been good talking to you."

<u>Its'</u> does not exist except as a mistake.

-IZE, LIKE and -WISE

-Ize

We start with a noun such as <u>minimum</u> and when we wish to say "make as small as possible," we think up the verb <u>to minimize</u>. We have an adjective such as <u>trivial</u> and when we want to say "reduce the significance of an idea," we invent the verb <u>trivialize</u>. We <u>sanitize</u>, we <u>scrutinize</u>, but should we be allowed to take any noun or adjective and fabricate verbs by adding -<u>ize</u> to the ends of these words? Words obtain legitimacy and are included in the dictionary because they are used a great deal. <u>Itemize</u> and <u>characterize</u> are two other nouns that have become verbs and there are many more. These new words tend to add vigor and flexibility to the language. But when you read the prose of outstanding writers, note that they avoid the practice of fabricating verbs from nouns and adjectives by adding -<u>ize</u> at the end. So it is not -<u>ize</u> be gone, but take a hint from the masters.

Like

<u>Like</u> is a fine verb. I <u>like</u> opera. <u>Like</u> serves also as a means of comparing, as in "It is like nothing I have ever seen." But <u>like</u> is a tiresome filler as in "They plan to put <u>like</u> a meat grinder in the corner," and "He <u>like</u> came over for a beer." <u>Like</u> be gone when used as a filler.

In the early 1970s, one could indicate one's trendy, leftist tendencies by inserting <u>like</u> into the conversation. The more the word could be inserted, the trendier, or more anti-establishment, or more to the left you were thought to be. Because the politics of the 1970s are a dead horse, and we have been told to stop beating dead horses, let's put <u>like</u> out to pasture. <u>Like</u> as a filler be gone.

-Wise

Could it have started with the word <u>otherwise</u>? This word derives from Old English <u>othre</u> <u>wisan</u>, meaning "in another manner." Now we add -<u>wise</u> to nouns such as <u>money</u>, <u>environment</u> and <u>nutrition</u>—perhaps to all nouns. We add -<u>wise</u> to <u>money</u> to make <u>moneywise</u>, as in "How are we moneywise?", meaning, "Are we broke?" And, "Environmentwise, the current administration has dropped the ball," meaning "The current administration is not protecting the environment." And, "He takes good care of himself nutritionwise," meaning "He has a healthy diet." The users of -<u>wise</u> as a general-purpose suffix may think that they have found a simple means of constructing sentences. Perhaps they have. To those who must listen to -<u>wise</u> but would never use it, the sound is worse than the fingernail on the blackboard. -<u>Wise</u> be gone.

LATER, LATTER and LATEST

Later. <u>Later</u> means "afterward" or "subsequently." If two events were mentioned, <u>later</u> refers to the one that occurred second. Its antonym is <u>earlier</u>.

> I hope to see you later.

> Let's go to a later performance.

> If the only possibilities are three p.m. and five p.m., I must select the later time.

Latter. <u>Latter</u> means "the second of two." It refers to the sequence in which two things or events were mentioned, which may not be the sequence in which they occurred. Its antonym is <u>former</u>.

> You ask me if I prefer carrots or cabbage. I prefer the latter.

> He broke out of jail and stole a lot of money. He performed the latter crime first and the former crime last.

Latest. <u>Latest</u> means "the most recent of three or more."

> The latest bulletin is encouraging.

LATIN ABBREVIATIONS

The list below contains many of the Latin abbreviations used commonly. Errors can be made in selecting the correct abbreviation. While the source may seem to be dated (1984), we are using a recently published version and, after all, Latin does not change.

Source: United States Government Printing Office
            Style Manual 1984 page 414

ad val., ad valorem	according to value
a.m., ante meridiem	before noon
c., circa	about
e.g., exempli gratia for	example
et al., et alibi	and elsewhere
et al., et alii	and others (masculine)
et aliae	and others (feminine)
etc., et cetera	and others, and so forth
et seq., et sequentes	and those that follow
hab. corp., habeas corpus	have the body—a writ
ib., ibid., ibidem	in the same place
i.e., id est	that is

N.B., nota bene	mark well
non seq., non sequitur	it does not follow logically
op. cit., opere citato	in the work cited
per se	<u>by</u>, <u>of</u>, or <u>in</u> itself (intrinsically)
P.M.,	post mortem after death
p.m., post meridiem	afternoon
Q.E.D., quod erat demonstrandum	which was to be demonstrated
s.d., sine die	indefinitely
v.g., verbi gratia	for example
viz, videlicet	namely
v.s., vide supra	see above

LIKE - AS

"Like" and "as" are used often in comparisons to say that something resembles something else. Here is how to avoid two common errors in their use.

A. **First common error.** When using "like" in a comparison, be sure that the object of "like" is a noun (or something equivalent to a noun, such as a pronoun or a gerund).

Here is a defective sentence:

Mary is very talented, <u>like her father says often</u>.

To understand the error in the sentence, let's see how "like" and "as" are used correctly in comparisons:

Mary is very talented, <u>like her father</u>.

Mary is very talented, <u>as her father says often</u>.

Both sentences B and C say that Mary is talented, but the first sentence implies that Mary's father is talented; the second sentence implies that he's proud of his daughter. "Like" is comparing two persons (Mary and her father), whereas "as" is comparing two statements ("Mary is very talented" and something that "her father says often"). Grammatically, "like" is a preposition, and the object of a preposition ("her father" in this case) is always a noun.

Now let's examine the defective sentence with which we started:

Mary is very talented, <u>like her father says often</u>.

In a subtle but important way, this sentence is ambiguous. It begins with "Mary is very talented, like . . . , " and the word "like" causes the reader to expect a noun as the object of the preposition "like." So when the sentence continues " . . . like her father," the reader assumes that Mary is being compared to her father. But then the sentence veers into " . . . her father says often," and the reader has to shift to a different interpretation, the interpretation that we readers must believe her father's assertion. The reader stumbles, consciously or unconsciously. You don't want your reader to stumble. Here are more examples of the same error:

Just do it, <u>like I showed you</u>.

<u>Like the weatherman predicted</u>, we had snow this morning.

He always makes his bed with hospital corners, <u>like in the Army</u>.

To avoid committing errors like these, be sure that the object of the proposition "like" is a noun or the equivalent of a noun. Here are some comparisons in which "like" and "as" are used correctly. Try to <u>hear</u> that the object of "like" is always a noun or the equivalent of a noun:

<u>Like Madonna</u>, she's a better performer than singer.

Just do it <u>as I showed you</u>.

Writing a story, <u>like composing a song</u>, requires patient revision.

<u>As the weatherman predicted</u>, we had snow this morning.

That's another weakness in your case, <u>like the fact that nobody but you saw the evidence</u>.

He always makes his bed with hospital corners, <u>as they require in the Army</u>.

He always makes his bed with hospital corners, <u>like an Army cot</u>.

Sometimes the narrator of a novel begins with a self-introduction, as in Melville's Moby Dick.

B.   Second common error. When using the "as . . . as" pattern, do not use the pronoun forms "me," "us," "him," "her," or "them" after the second "as." If you use one of these pronouns, use the form "I," "we," "he," "she," or "they."

Here are two sentences that use the "as . . . as" pattern incorrectly:

She's as tall <u>as me</u>.

I'm as strong <u>as him</u>.

And here are some sentences that use the pattern correctly:

She's as tall <u>as I</u>.

I'm as strong <u>as she</u>.

We're as welcome <u>as they are</u>.

The error occurs only when you use certain pronouns after the second "as." These pronouns take different forms (cases), depending upon whether they're used as subjects or objects. If the pronoun is the <u>subject</u> of a verb ("I saw Benny"), it takes the <u>nominative</u> form "I," "we," "he," "she," or "they." If it's the object of a verb ("Benny saw me") or of a preposition ("It was beside me"), it takes the <u>accusative</u> form "me," "us," "him," "her," or "them."

When you use one of these pronouns after the second "as" in the "as . . . as" pattern, give it the nominative form:

She's as tall <u>as I</u>.

I'm as strong <u>as he</u>. (or "as he is.")

If you've been following the discussion closely, you might object here, "You said that these pronouns take the nominative case when they're the subject of the verb. But in 'She's as tall as I,' how is 'I' the subject of a verb? Where's the verb?"

The verb is <u>understood</u>. The second "as" is followed by a statement, part of which is unspoken: "She's as tall as I[am tall]," "I'm as strong as he [is strong]." In other words, "as I" and "as he" are something like abbreviations for "as I am tall" and "as he is strong."

So when you're not sure which form of the pronoun to use, complete the understood clause in your head. You wouldn't say "She's as tall as me am tall" or "I'm as strong as he is strong." Instead, you'd say "She's as tall as I am tall," etc. So write "She's as tall as I (or "She's as tall as I am") and "I'm as strong as he (or "I'm as strong as he is").

NOT ONLY BUT ALSO

Sentences that contain <u>not only</u> should also contain <u>but also</u> for balance and power. There is no rule of grammar that says <u>not only</u> must be followed by <u>but also</u>, but in formal English writing, that sequence extracts the power available in the sentence. Here are examples of sentences that might be called incomplete because while they have <u>not only</u>, they contain <u>but</u> in place of <u>but also</u>, or no <u>but also</u> at all, as in this first example.

"These three men should be capable of this not only as a matter of favorable calculation vis-à-vis their own chances." The sentence needs a clause starting with <u>but also</u> in order to complete the writer's thoughts.

"During the campaign, the candidate promised not only to shield the middle class from tax increases but to cut their taxes." The sentence needs an <u>also</u> after <u>but</u>. (During the campaign, the candidate promised not only to shield the middle class from tax increases but also to cut their taxes.)

PERIOD AND TIME

About twenty years ago, some people in public life started to use the expression "at this point in time." From that moment, all hell broke loose. New phrases were introduced to describe the passage of time and the word "period" became overused. Here are a few combinations and the word(s) each replaced.

A. Period

Interim Period
Interim is a noun meaning "the passage of a certain amount of time," "an interval." If a company, as an example, finds itself without a chief executive for a few months, one can say "In the interim, the company was run by the department heads." No need to say "interim period."

Period of Time or Time Period
Period has two meanings. The first meaning is to indicate a punctuation mark. The second meaning is to denote the passage of time in situations that repeat themselves such as the time required for a pendulum to go through one cycle or an engine to go through one revolution. Period of time is a redundant expression. Period means the passage of time. How can we say, passage of time of time?

Solution? Say "how much time," "amount of time," or "the time required." As an example, in place of asking "what period of time will you need to get ready?" ask "how much time will you need to get ready?" If no repetition is indicated, do not use the word period. One hears "During that five-year period of drought, many crops failed." Say instead "During those five years of drought, many crops failed."

Relatively Short Period of Time

Say shortly, or soon. "He labored under the heavy load and in a relatively short period of time he became tired." It is simpler to say "He labored under the heavy load and became tired soon."

Transition Period

"The report states that there will be a transition period of three to five years." A transition is time during which change takes place. No need to add period. The sentence can read "The report states that there will be a transition lasting three to five years."

Some amount of time followed by the word period

"The trustees will be elected for the three-year period ending in the fall of 1996." No need to insert period into the sentence. It can read "The trustees will be elected for the three years ending in the fall of 1999."

So much for the incorrect use of that over-used word period. The word time has been in for abuse as well in the past decade. Here are some samples of time finding itself associated with other words to the detriment of clarity.

B. Time

Point in Time

If talking about the present, as in "At this point in time, we are at war with two countries," say instead "We are at war with two countries now." If talking about the past, as in "At that point in time, gas was very expensive," say instead "Gas was very expensive then." Now and then have become under-utilized, having been replaced by that weed point in time. Time for the weed-killer.

Time Frame

Frame as in time frame could have come from the movies. Each still shot that makes up a motion picture (there are twenty-four frames per second in a commercial motion picture) is called a frame. Time frame would be a useful addition to the language if we were not blessed with the word <u>when</u> to express the same thought. Instead of asking "What's the <u>time frame</u> for finishing the report?" one may as well ask "When will you finish the report?"

Time Line

A <u>time line</u> is a graph which denotes events and the dates they occurred. One can construct a time line by placing the Earth's geological eras along a straight line representing the Earth's four-billion-year life, and noting the date of each era. <u>Time line</u> does not mean "schedule," nor does it mean "time elapsed." Do not ask "What's your time line for finishing the project?" Instead, ask "How much time will you need to finish the project?"

Time horizon

"People should have at least a five-year time horizon if they invest in stocks." A more precise version than the above might read as follows: "People should wait five years before evaluating the final results of investing in stocks."

Here is another example: "Old people tend to buy more bonds than stocks and this habit reflects a shortened time horizon." There are two comments to make about this sentence. The first is that horizons are nearer or farther away, not shorter or longer. If you don't believe that to be the case, look out the window. The second is that the writer wants to tell us that old individuals tend to buy assets that pay predictable interest and dividends rather than growth stocks that pay neither. The sentence might be written, "Old people tend to buy more Treasury bonds than high-technology stocks and this habit reflects their need for a secure, predictable income."

Time spectrum

<u>Spectrum</u> is a technical word describing an array of continuously varying wavelengths. When we look at a rainbow, we see the spectrum of the visible range of electro-magnetic radiation. When used in a non-scientific way, as in the phrase "Smith was not certain of the time spectrum," readers know that Smith is

confused, but then, so are they. Combining <u>time</u> and <u>spectrum</u> can only lead to uncertainty.

Time sequence

"As I look back on that day, I am no longer aware of the time sequence of events." The sentence is clear. The speaker no longer remembers the order in which events happened. <u>Sequence</u> describes the order in which events follow one another. No need to add <u>time</u>. The sentence should read "As I look back on that day, I am no longer aware of the sequence of events."

Time span

"In the time span of sixty years, the welfare state has come full circle." No need to say <u>time</u>. "In the span of sixty years, the welfare state has come full circle." Or, "In the last sixty years, the welfare state has come full circle." Both are acceptable.

Time limit

"There now only remains a five-year time limit for welfare benefits." No need to say <u>time</u>. The meaning of "five-year limit" is clear.

Space of time

"In the space of time we have left . . ." No need to say <u>space</u>. Say instead "In the time we have left . . ."

PUNCTUATION

No comments are made here about the use of commas, semicolons, and periods. Educated people make few mistakes when using these punctuation marks. It appears, however, that many writers fail to identify acronyms by placing them within parentheses right after the complete words that they stand for, and many writers, not necessarily the same ones, use the virgule incorrectly. Here is a discussion of these two art forms.

A. Parentheses to Identify Acronyms

When writing a column about an organization with a long name such as the Democratic Leadership Council, a journalist might wish to use in subsequent references the acronym DLC in place of the three words, <u>Democratic</u> <u>Leadership</u> <u>Council</u>. How to do this? After writing the full name the first time, write the three initials (the acronym) in parentheses immediately afterwards, as follows:

"The Democratic Leadership Council (DLC) has published policy statements on many issues."

If the journalist writes "Democratic Leadership Council" and then writes a paragraph or two before using the acronym, the reader might have to stop and go back in the article to find out the meaning of the initials. When the journalist places the initials in parentheses immediately after the first use of the complete name, the reader is told to watch for the acronym later in the text.

B. Virgule

The virgule is the right-slanting diagonal (/). It has uses in punctuation such as a substitute for <u>per</u> in describing rates (20 ft./hr. for 20 feet per hour) and in separating years (1988/89). The virgule is also used to separate alternatives as in <u>and/or</u>. It is in this use that writers make mistakes. Here is an example of a writer falling into said trap: "Each horse/rider combination must complete all phases of the competition." The writer did not mean "each horse or rider . . . , " the writer meant "each combination of horse and rider . . . , " or, "each horse-rider combination." Put that virgule back in its stall. The same error occurs when writers discuss the relationship that exists between lawyers and clients as in the phrase "lawyer/client privilege" when they ought to write "lawyer-client privilege."

Another common error that writers make is to use the virgule to indicate an abbreviation such as T/P for <u>taxpayer</u>. This is a new and groundless application for this punctuation mark. If you mean <u>taxpayer</u>, do not abbreviate by writing T/P; write <u>taxpayer</u>.

Do not use the virgule to separate a series of nouns or adjectives when the spoken separation between them is <u>and</u>. As an example, it is incorrect to write "That mutt was mean/dirty/angry and the perfect junk-yard guard dog." Write, "That mutt was mean, dirty and angry. He was the perfect junk-yard guard dog."

Use the virgule to separate nouns and adjectives only when separating alternatives. The dictionary gives an example of adjectives separated by a virgule from prose by William Saroyan: " . . . sit hour after hour . . . and finally year after year in a catatonic/frenzied trance rewriting the Bible."

SEQUENCE

There is usually one sequence for placing the words in a sentence that will not cause the reader to slow down in order to discern the meaning.

As a general guideline to sequencing, put together words and phrases that belong together. Writers may not be able to spot bad sequences right away, but 24 hours after they have been written, they jump off the page directly at the writer. Reread and revise scrupulously.

Here are examples of sentences that contain a word or a phrase that is not in the most logical sequence. An improved version is in parentheses.

"The author brings small details of history to light." (The author brings to light small details of history.)

"Each allowable exemption will reduce the income that would otherwise be taxed by $2,350." (Here is how the sentence should read: "Each allowable exemption will reduce by $2,350 the income that is taxed." Note that <u>otherwise</u> is not needed when the sequence is changed.)

"But the tides that were being raised began to slow both Earth and Moon down, not much at first, . . ." (But the tides that were being raised began to slow down both the Earth and Moon, not much at first, . . .)

"There is an anthology containing excerpts from the works of sixteen great authors in order to illustrate how the masters write the language." (Excerpts from the works of sixteen great authors are presented as an anthology in order to illustrate how the masters write the language.)

"Copy comes to your desk from reporters for review." (Copy from reporters comes to your desk for review.)

" . . . cutting the time it takes to cross the Pacific in half . . ." (. . . cutting in half the time it takes to cross the Pacific . . . .)

"Disgruntled voters may sit this election out." (Disgruntled voters may sit out this election.)

"It's important to pick this stuff up." (It's important to pick up this stuff.)

"When we say we have a word about Washington to express . . ." (When we say we have a word to express about Washington . . .)

"You have to supply all the energy required to get over the inertia that all of us have in order to get the job done." (In order to get the job done, you have to supply all the energy required to get over the inertia that all of us have.)

"The Congress voted temporarily to increase the debt limit." (The Congress voted to increase the debt limit temporarily.)

" . . . for failing adequately to supervise one of its employees." (. . . for failing to supervise one of its employees adequately.)

UNIQUE

"Unique" is an adjective meaning "being the only one" or "being without a like or equal." When the meaning is written out, one sees that the word "Unique" cannot be modified. It makes no sense to say "very unique," "somewhat unique," "totally unique," or "truly unique."

Take the pledge—never modify <u>unique</u> again.

WEEDS

Weeds are phrases or words that add no meaning to a sentence. Listen to yourself, or reread your material, identify those weeds, and yank them. The weeds in these examples have been underlined.

"He kind of dropped in for dinner." Forget kind of.

"Tax increases are not some sort of a panacea for the budget deficits." So long, some sort of.

"I don't know if I have ever had that big of a pain." Amputate of.

"Where is the building at?" Get that "at" out of there. This sentence could be an example of redundancy. "Where" and "at" both indicate location.

"To be sure, the statistics could be questioned." Goodbye, to be sure. Those three words add nothing to the sentence.

"First of all, the sand was hot. Second of all, we had no shoes." Drop of all. "First, the sand was hot, and second, we had no shoes." The second version packs more punch than the first.

"You know, we play as a team. The individual performance doesn't count. You know what I mean?" Yank those two weeds, you know and you know what I mean.

"The thing of it is, the house is too big for us." The thing of it is is a substitute for "you know what I mean" and deserves the same fate.

Here are a few sentences whose weeds are underlined. No need to rewrite each sentence without its weed.

"The recommendations apply to men as well as women, though most single parents are <u>of course</u> mothers."

"Yet some independent scholars are coming to <u>rather</u> different conclusions."

"She tried to check on the grades of the second-year student in order to assess her level of <u>actual</u> skill."

"As president of the company, he is ultimately responsible for the quality of the <u>manufactured</u> products."

"The writing task was <u>simply</u> assigned to one of the staff."

"Such moves would be painful and politically difficult <u>no matter what</u>."

"Charlie Adams' success illustrates the <u>kind of</u> impact he is having throughout the country."

WHAT

The word <u>what</u> has its place in speaking and writing. Inappropriate use of the word, however, can cause havoc in sentences. Here are sentences containing <u>what</u> as they appeared in their original form, followed by rewritten versions that are shorter and clearer than the originals.

"Charlie reports that environmental policy changes are <u>what</u> most of the people he has talked to are very apprehensive about." (Try this version: Charlie reports that most people whom he has talked to are very apprehensive about changes in environmental policy.)

"The root of the country's economic problems lies in insufficient private investment, and what impedes private investment most is a legal system that does not enforce private contracts." (The root of the country's economic problems consists of insufficient private investment which is impeded most by a legal system that does not enforce private contracts.)

"What no doubt worries Lithuanians most is their inability to fashion the break from the former USSR more to their own liking." (Lithuanians worry most about their inability to fashion to their liking the break from the former USSR.) In this version, we have removed what, no doubt and own. We have reversed the order of from the former USSR and to their own liking which adds punch to the sentence.)

"We don't have a lot of clues to what the CEO and his legal advisor will come up with." (The CEO and his legal advisor have not revealed their plans.)

"I was not happy, although what Morgan said was clearly right." (I was not happy, although Morgan told us the truth.)

"She has done interesting work about what images mean." (She has done interesting work about the meaning of images.)

" . . . would determine each year <u>what</u> reports should be examined and <u>what</u> type of examination should be conducted." (. . . would determine each year which reports should be examined and which type of examination should be conducted)

On occasion, a sentence starting with <u>what</u> suggests to the reader that there will be a question mark at the end. When the reader finds none, surprise sets in. Re-reading takes place. Time is lost. Concentration is broken. Here is such a sentence.

"Put another way, <u>what</u> is a significant reduction in the size of long-term offerings represents a moderate addition to short-term financing." As written, the entire clause from <u>what</u> through <u>offerings</u> is the subject of the verb represents. A reader who is looking for a question mark after seeing what, and finds none when arriving at represents, is knocked for a loop. Write the sentence this way: "Put another way, a significant reduction in the size of long-term offerings represents a moderate addition to short-term financing."

We can shorten many sentences for efficiency and rewrite many for clarity. Sentences containing <u>what</u> are often candidates for rewriting.

EDITING—TRY YOUR HAND

You are an editor who works at a daily newspaper or a weekly magazine. Copy from reporters arrives at your desk for review. You may allow the copy to be printed as-is, or you may make some changes.

Here are sentences and phrases that we have taken from recent publications. They appear at random. These selections are grammatically correct and comprehensible as they stand. Would you change them? Try your hand at editing. We give our suggestion for an improved version in the section that follows, keeping the selections in the same sequence in both the original and modified versions.

Even though the sentences are grammatically correct, we have changed either the subject or the verb, or some aspect of the sentence. Our purpose in making these changes is to ensure that there are no reporters whose material we read who can conclude that we are finding fault with their writing. We are not finding fault. We are playing editor (playing at being editor).

1. Excited at the prospect of winning, she hand-delivered her essay to the committee.

2. If the adverbs remain in the middle of the verbs, much of what can be got out of these sentences is lost.

3. Charles' values seemed out of keeping with what most people in town regard as appropriate.

4. It became immediately obvious.

5. The executives determine on what policies to put in place.

6. Wealth creation . . . .

7. The problem was the way they insisted on flying in bad weather.

8. But absent the global struggle between haves and have-nots . . . .

9. The anti-liberty demagogues well understand that their cause will lose in the end.

10. As the legislature prepares to formally take up the bill . . . .

11. A clue to what has gone wrong in the space program is provided by looking at what has happened to the engineering profession over the past fifteen years.

12. This is not primarily due to any difference in their strength.

13. His attempt to reach the top is testimony to the fact that he will not permit himself to fail.

14. Ultra-conservatism derives what energy it has from political thinking of the last century.

15. Pacifists have the opportunity now to question the very purpose of some portions of our armed forces.

16. A taxpayer may claim medical expenses paid for a parent who would have qualified as the taxpayer's dependent except for the fact that the parent's gross income exceeded $2,350.

17. American optimism about the future . . . .

18. It will be up to the bishop to ultimately determine.

19. He is a great talent.

20. Only a fraction of these sites has been cleaned up.

21. I did not like him going away.

22. The museum wishes to continue having quality exhibition scheduling.

23. Somebody is going to have to carry the water up the hill.

24. The soldiers did not eat all that well during the winter.

25. The manager of the building refuses to even allow small, quiet pets such as cats.

26. There is no chief of staff who is going to be able to head off escalating costs.

27. This report is basically designed to inform the staff.

28. The runner was particularly outstanding.

29. He had lunch every day at a prestige private club.

30. . . . to really understand . . . to fully invest . . . to truly want . . . to actually achieve . . .

31. Scientists do not venture beyond the known facts.

32. For the first time, the CEO makes the decisions, not committees.

33. The problems faced by the nation can be solved only over a period of time.

34. A meeting held at the Center for Disease Control determined that most of the diseases common to children a century ago are controlled by immunization.

35. Interest rates rose a full percentage point yesterday.

EDITING—AUTHORS' VERSIONS

1. Excited at the prospect of winning, she delivered her essay to the committee in person. (<u>In person</u> is a substitute for the slang expression <u>hand-delivered</u>.)

2. If the adverbs remain in the middle of the verbs, the power in these sentences is lost. (The long phrase, <u>much of what can be got out of</u>, can be replaced by the noun, <u>power</u>.)

3. Charles' values seemed out of keeping with those of most people in town. (A phrase beginning with <u>what</u> can be shortened frequently.)

4. It was obvious. (<u>Obvious</u> means "easily discovered, seen, or understood." If one can discern the meaning of a situation at a glance, no need to add <u>immediately</u>.)

5. The executives determine which policies to put in place. (Both <u>what</u> and <u>which</u> are correct; however, <u>which</u> means, "what one out of a group," and appears to fit better than <u>what</u>.)

6. Creation of wealth. (Avoid using a noun, <u>wealth</u> in this case, as an adjective unless the two-word or three-word combination is entrenched firmly in the lexicon. As an example, we say <u>dog house</u>, and no one says <u>house of the dog</u>. Some reporters and writers take all opportunities to turn nouns into adjectives by not using the preposition <u>of</u>. An editor might inject a judicious <u>of</u> from time to time to break up the writer's pattern.)

7. The problem was caused by their insistence on flying in bad weather. (The words, <u>was the way they</u>, lend themselves to misinterpretation. Was the problem the fashion in which these

aviators insisted, or was the problem that these aviators insisted on flying in bad weather? The version here assumes the latter.)

8. Without the global struggle between the haves and have-nots . . . . (<u>Absent</u> is an adjective or a transitive verb, and rarely a preposition. Use of <u>absent</u> in this instance can confuse readers.)

9. The anti-liberty demagogues understand that their cause will lose in the end. (The adverb <u>well</u>, modifying the verb, <u>understand</u>, might be placed after the verb, but <u>understand well</u> does not appear familiar to the reader. If an adverb is needed, then say, <u>understand fully</u>.)

10. As the legislature prepares to take up the bill . . . . (Readers cannot distinguish between <u>formally taking up</u> and <u>taking up</u>. Do legislatures spend time <u>informally taking up</u> bills? Eliminate <u>formally</u>.)

11. A clue to identifying the problems in the space program is provided by identifying the changes in the engineering profession over the past fifteen years. (The clause, <u>what has gone wrong</u>, can be changed to <u>identifying the problems</u>. Clauses starting with <u>what</u> can be awkward.)

12. This is not due primarily to any difference in their strength. (Move the adverb, <u>primarily</u>, from a spot in the middle of the verb to the end of the verb.)

13. His attempt to reach the top demonstrates that he will not permit himself to fail. (The phrase, <u>is testimony to the fact that</u>, can be shortened to the verb, <u>demonstrates</u>.)

14. Ultra-conservatism derives its energy from political thinking of the last century. (The clause beginning with <u>what</u> can be shortened.)

15. Pacifists have the opportunity now to question the purpose of some portions of our armed forces. (<u>Very</u> as a modifier to <u>purpose</u> does not add meaning to the sentence.)

16. A taxpayer may claim medical expenses paid for a parent who would have qualified as the taxpayer's dependent had not the parent's gross income exceeded $2,350. (The phrase, <u>except for the fact that</u>, can be replaced by the phrase, <u>had not</u>, in order to save words. If a reporter uses <u>except for</u> frequently, <u>but for</u> can be substituted from time to time by the editor.)

17. American optimism . . . . (It is difficult to be optimistic about the past.)

18. Here are three ways of re-writing this sentence:
    It will be up to the bishop to determine.
    It will be up to the bishop to determine ultimately.
    In the end, it will be up to the bishop to determine.
    (In the original version, the infinitive, <u>to determine</u>, was split by the adverb, <u>ultimately</u>.)

19. He has a great talent. (A talent is a trait that one possesses, a natural endowment. A talent is not a trait that describes a person such as the words, <u>large</u> or <u>smart</u>. One <u>is</u> large, or smart, but one is not a talent. One has talent.)

20. Only a fraction of these sites have been cleaned up. (The subject of the verb is the collective noun <u>fraction</u> which is assumed to be plural because it refers to several sites. In the sentence: "Only a fraction of the damage has been cleaned up," note that the verb is in the singular form because <u>damage</u> does not represent several objects, but rather a single concept or situation.)

21. I did not like his going away. (<u>Going</u> ends in <u>ing</u> and is used here as a noun, and therefore it is a gerund. The word preceding the gerund must be in the possessive case. In place of <u>him going</u>, the correct form is <u>his going</u>.)

22. The museum wishes to continue scheduling exhibitions of high quality. (While the three-noun sequence, <u>quality exhibition scheduling</u>, provides the meaning desired by the writer, one can break up the sequence as is done above and the adjective <u>high</u> can

be added to modify <u>quality</u>. We do not know whether the coming exhibitions will be of low, medium, or high quality without the appropriate adjective.)

23. Somebody must carry the water up the hill. (<u>must</u> is shorter than <u>going to have to</u> and means the same.)

24. The soldiers did not eat well during the winter. (<u>All that</u> is an implied comparison, so that <u>all that well</u> could mean that the soldiers did not eat as well as civilians, or as well as sailors, or as well as soldiers eat in the summer. Because the meaning of <u>all that</u> is not clear, we vote to take it out.)

25. The manager of the building refuses to allow even small, quiet pets such as cats. (Place the adverb, <u>even</u>, after the verb in order to avoid splitting the infinitive, <u>to allow</u>. The sentence reads well without <u>even</u>, so, as an alternative, it can be left out.)

26. There is no chief of staff who can head off escalating costs. (<u>Can</u> is a substitute for <u>is going to be able to</u>.)

27. This report is designed to inform the staff. (<u>Basically</u> adds no meaning to the sentence.)

28. The runner was outstanding. (To describe a person or a performance as <u>outstanding</u> places the individual or the performance at the top of the heap. No need to add the adverb, <u>particularly</u>.)

29. He had lunch every day at a prestigious private club. (<u>Prestige</u> is a noun. <u>Prestigious</u> is the adjectival form.)

30. In the original clauses, the infinitives <u>to understand</u>, <u>to invest</u>, <u>to want</u> and <u>to achieve</u> are split by the adverbs <u>really</u>, <u>fully</u>, <u>truly</u>, and <u>actually</u>. Three of these adverbs, <u>really</u>, <u>truly</u>, and <u>actually</u> add no meaning and can be eliminated. The adverb <u>fully</u> should be kept because one can be <u>invest partially</u>, as an example, but the adverb should be placed after the infinitive, <u>to invest fully</u>.

31. Scientists do not venture beyond the facts. (The past participle, <u>known</u>, is not required to convey the meaning intended. Unknown facts are scarce.)

32. For the first time, the CEO, not committees, makes the decisions. (The sequence shown here is clearer than the sequence in the original version.)

33. The problems faced by the nation can be solved only over time. (<u>Period of time</u> is a built-in redundancy. The word <u>period</u> signifies some amount of time and the notion that the passage of time is repetitive, as in the motion of a pendulum.)

34. A meeting held at the Center for Disease Control (CDC) determined that most of the diseases common to children a century ago are controlled by immunization. (In the article that this sentence is taken from, the Center for Disease Control is referred to several times and the acronym, CDC, is used without having identified it immediately after the first use of the name, Center for Disease Control. By the way, the article, although it referred to the Center for Disease Control, did not discuss children's diseases of a century ago. The text is changed here to place camouflage around the author and the article.)

35. Interest rates rose a percentage point yesterday. (Adding the adjective <u>full</u> is not necessary.)

ANTHOLOGY

COMMENTS ON WRITING
CONTENTS OF THE ANTHOLOGY

COMMENTS ON WRITING

Two hundred years ago Samuel Johnson wrote that "whoever wishes to attain an English style, familiar but not coarse, and elegant but not ostentatious, must give his days and nights to the volumes of Addison." This is still good advice. We learn much from the masters.

The pages that follow contain passages of contemporary English prose which we believe illustrate the cardinal virtues of brevity, clarity, and power, from which come style. By "contemporary," we mean the language that has been spoken and written by educated people, as they use formal English, over the last two hundred years. Informal English, spoken by all ranks of society under the various circumstances that are experienced in daily life, changes daily. Formal English, from Jefferson forward, has not changed a great deal.

A word about brevity. Writers and speakers launch forth with the objective of persuading readers and listeners concerning a particular point of view. Brevity to these performers is the knack of using only those words and structures required to carry the argument to the reader and listener. All else is superfluous. Brevity does not mean to cut it short. It does mean that there is not an extra word, phrase, sentence, paragraph or thought. As you read the excerpts that follow, be aware of the sparseness. A beautiful garden contains the number of plants and flowers required to create the desired impression. There is no superfluous planting. There are no weeds.

Concerning clarity. Words are the clothes of thought. While we can experience fear, cold, and hunger without a vocabulary to describe these emotions, we cannot think about politics, religion, economics and science without clothing them in the vocabulary specific to each of these disciplines. We must employ words that match the concepts. Clarity is derived from the use of words that convey the exact meanings that authors intend. The works of great authors live, in part, because the authors have selected the most precise words for the occasions.

On power. Power is built on clarity. Power is clarity refined. The writer must be meticulous in arranging thoughts and actions in the most logical sequence so that the reader can absorb the message without interruption, paragraphs at a time. Any break in the logic or the sequence breaks the reader's attention. If a reader stops in mid-paragraph and asks, "what did I miss?" or "what does this mean?" then the writer lost the reader, perhaps only for a moment, but the power inherent in the work has evaporated.

Power comes as well from using bold, stark phrases that create powerful images in the minds of readers and listeners. After Dunkirk, Churchill said in Parliament, " . . . we shall fight on the beaches, we shall fight on the landing grounds, we shall fight in the fields and in the streets, we shall fight in the hills; we shall never surrender;" Martin Luther King, Jr. summed up his hopes for America by saying in his Lincoln Memorial speech "I have a dream . . ." And Lincoln said "The ballot is stronger than the bullet." Powerful words move people to action at the time they are spoken or written and they maintain their power for years afterwards. Generations over twenty centuries have been affected by these words, " . . . and forgive us our trespasses as we forgive those who trespass against us."

Finally, style. There can be no style without brevity, clarity, and power. Style, that extra ingredient, comes from an understanding of the fundamental elements that make up the topic under discussion, and the connections among the elements, and the connection between the topic and the world in which the topic exists. In <u>For Whom The Bell Tolls</u>, Hemingway's hero, Robert Jordan, becomes a member of a band of guerrillas fighting in the Spanish Civil War. Hemingway understands the people Jordan lives and fights with, and the enemy, and the issues of the war. He understands the people and events so well that he can explain them to the reader, he can take the reader to the scene. The novel is not a commentary on that civil war, it is an opportunity to relive it. In <u>Babbitt</u>, Sinclair Lewis gives us a complete expose of the small-town, mid-western personality. You know he knows it. There is nothing else to be known about it. He does not comment on it. He explains it. That must be at the heart of good writing, that thirst for explaining something so clearly, that desire to bring the message to the reader, that urge to carry the reader to the scene, to do all those things so well that they cannot be improved upon.

Style is precisely like beauty: it is in the mind of the beholder. You read a piece and are struck by its simplicity, depth of understanding, clarity of thought, selection of words, and emotional impact, and you say, "That's beautiful." The appreciation of another's style is not something you can see or touch. It is something that touches you. Style does not come only from the great authors, although they have it, or their works would not have lived. Style can come, as an example, from a reporter who understands the significance of events and is able to write about them from the heart. Style is simple, that is to say, it represents complex thoughts reduced to their elements. Style is reserved neither for the brilliant nor for the best educated among us. Style can and does come from those whom we call simple people when it is their turn to relate an emotion or an event having significance to them, be it in a letter, or in simple discourse, or in a speech. As people devoted to a craft, writers know that their natural style will work itself to the surface by the dedication required of this and all crafts, and by events in their lives which made accessible to them the deepest emotions that we experience.

Read the excerpts that follow for pleasure. We think that the passages have special merit: They exhibit brevity, clarity, power, and style. The reader will not find that these passages are long-winded, unclear, unpersuasive, and lacking in style.

Good writing is a reflection of humanness. Brevity is prized in all things. Time is precious. Clarity is mandatory in the affairs of man. The lack of it is so costly. Power is valued. We must shape opinions, persuade others, get things done. And finally, style and beauty are our means of attaining perfection. Perfection in anything is the one natural goal. Because humans maintain the same requirements of good writing in the formal language over the centuries, good writing does not change. Plutarch wrote interesting biographies nineteen hundred years ago. His work is as fresh and entertaining today as then. No Academy is needed to keep the formal language from going astray.

We close with this thought, that great writers and speakers elect not to commit the frequently-made errors that are the subject of the earlier part of this text. As they learned the craft of putting thoughts and actions to paper, these people who deal with words learned the rules of grammar, the arrangement of phrases, a massive vocabulary, and the spelling of it. These experts, or practitioners, or whatever we choose to call them, constitute our academy. It is they, by the successful application of the language, who determine what is and what is not acceptable. There are no absolutes in language. It is to the most successful, the most profound, that we turn for guidance. When we read something and say, "My, that's good writing," then that is the language.

CONTENTS OF THE ANTHOLOGY

Ulysses S. Grant, <u>Personal Memoirs of U.S. Grant</u>, recounting the surrender of General R. E. Lee at Appomattox Court House in 1865, Charles L. Webster & Co., New York, 1885.

Thomas Jefferson, First Inaugural Address, two letters (to Captain Meriwether Lewis, to Monsieur Sylvestre in Paris), and three of the four inscriptions in the Jefferson Memorial in Washington, D.C. The first inaugural address and the letters are contained in <u>The Writings of Thomas Jefferson</u>, Thomas Jefferson Memorial Association of the United States, 1904.

Abraham Lincoln, excerpts from a speech, "The Perpetuation of our Political Institutions," given before the Young Men's Lyceum, Springfield, Illinois, January 27, 1838; excerpts from a speech, "Military Tail of the Great Michigander," given in the House of Representatives, July 27, 1848; letter to Horace Greeley, August 22, 1862. All materials are taken from <u>The Collected Works of Abraham Lincoln</u>, Roy P. Basler, editor, Rutgers University Press, New Brunswick, New Jersey, 1953.

Thomas Macaulay, <u>History of England from the Accession of James II</u>, E. H. Butler & Co., Philadelphia, 1856.

Plutarch, excerpt from the Life of Julius Caesar, taken from <u>The Lives of the Noble Grecians and Romans</u>, translated by John Dryden (1683-1686) and revised by Arthur Hugh Clough (1864, 1876), the Modern Library, Random House, Inc., New York.

Leo Tolstoy, <u>War and Peace</u>, translated by Louise and Aylmer Maude, Simon and Shuster, New York 1942.

ULYSSES S. GRANT

Personal Memoirs of U. S. Grant
Charles L. Webster & Co.
New York, 1885

Ulysses S. Grant was a soldier, politician and writer. The customary reaction to Grant's military career, the brilliant end of it, is surprise that it happened. He graduated from West Point in 1843, served in the army throughout the Mexican War and resigned his commission (he had reached the rank of captain) in 1854. He gave as reason for his resignation that he could not support his wife and two children on army pay. He returned to the army in 1861, and under the direction of the governor of Illinois, he organized regiments of infantry, taking command of the twenty-first as a colonel of Illinois Volunteers. His rise in rank, stature and importance were meteoric: he became the first lieutenant general since Washington and, after the Civil War, the first four-star general.

Countries turn to war heroes for filling high political offices. Grant remained in the service after the war as commander-in-chief of the army and was elected president to the first of his two terms in 1868, taking office 4 March 1869.

Grant published his memoirs in 1885, a year before his death. They were a financial success. The clarity of the prose, the great interest in the subject matter, the arresting vignettes, and the occasional insights into the character of others, are the reasons that this war story holds the reader's attention.

The third paragraph of the selection brings together Grant's thoughts about Lee and his own opinion on the Civil War. He guesses at Lee's emotions, and then discusses his own at the moment of surrender. He gives his opinion of the cause over which the war was fought. Finally,

Grant admits his understanding that the Southern people, though wrong, as he saw it, could hold the view that they did and be willing to fight for it. These words, " . . . though that cause was, I believe, one of the worst for which a people fought, and one for which there was the least excuse. I do not question, however, the sincerity of the great mass of those who were opposed to us." These words bring together Grant's feelings about the war and the people whom he fought. They appear to sum up the Civil War in his mind.

In his autobiography, Grant surprises us once again. The two-volume opus starts with a short discourse on his childhood, his years at West Point, and then rolls on in a clear, simple, declaratory style. It is interesting and informative. Though not trained as a writer, Grant appears to treat writing his memoirs as he did any other campaign—head down, straight ahead toward the objective. It was his last campaign.

The selection is taken from volume 2, pages 488 through 491. The events take place on April 9, 1865.

I had known General Lee in the old army and had served with him in the Mexican War; but did not suppose, owing to the difference in our age and rank, that he would remember me; while I would more naturally remember him distinctly, because he was the chief of staff of General Scott in the Mexican War.

When I left camp that morning I had not expected so soon the result that was then taking place, and consequently was in rough garb. I was without a sword, as I usually was when on horseback on the field, and wore a soldier's blouse for a coat, with the shoulder straps of my rank to indicate to the army who I was. When I went into the house I found General Lee. We greeted each other, and after shaking hands took our seats. I had my staff with me, a good portion of whom were in the room during the whole interview.

What General Lee's feelings were I do not know. As he was a man of much dignity, with an impassible face, it was impossible to say whether he felt inwardly glad that the end had finally come, or felt sad over the result, and was too manly to show it. Whatever his feelings, they were entirely concealed from my observation; but my own feelings, which had been quite jubilant on the receipt of his letter, were sad and depressed. I felt like anything rather than rejoicing at the downfall of a foe who had fought so long and valiantly, and had suffered so much for a cause, though that cause was, I believe, one of the worst for which a people ever fought, and one for which there was the least excuse. I do not question, however, the sincerity of the great mass of those who were opposed to us.

General Lee was dressed in a full uniform which was entirely new, and was wearing a sword of considerable value, very likely the sword which had been presented by the State of Virginia; at all events, it was an entirely different sword from the one that would ordinarily be worn in the field. In my rough traveling suit, the uniform of a private with the straps of a lieutenant-general, I must have contrasted very strangely with a man so handsomely dressed, six feet high and of faultless form. But this is not a matter that I thought of until afterwards.

We soon fell into conversation about old army times. He remarked that he remembered me very well in the old army; and I told him that as a matter of course I remembered him perfectly, but from the difference in our rank and years (there being about sixteen years' difference in our ages), I had thought it very likely that I had not attracted his attention sufficiently to be remembered by him after such a long interval. Our conversation grew so pleasant that I almost forgot the object of our meeting. After the conversation had run in this style for some time, General Lee called my attention to the object of our meeting, and said that he had asked for this interview for the purpose of getting from me the terms I proposed to give his army. I said that I meant merely that his army should lay down their arms, not take them up again during the continuance of the war unless duly and properly exchanged. He said that he had so understood my letter.

Then we gradually fell off again into conversation about matters foreign to the subject which had brought us together. This continued for some little time, when General Lee again interrupted the course of the conversation by suggesting that the terms I propose to give his army ought to be written out. I called to General Parker, secretary on my staff, for writing materials, and commenced writing out the following terms:

Appomattox C.H., Va.,
Apl 9th, 1865

Gen. R. E. Lee,
Comd'g C.S.A.

Gen: In accordance with the substance of my letter to you of the 8th inst., I propose to receive the surrender of the Army of N. Va. on the following terms, to wit: Rolls of all the officers and men to be made in duplicate. One copy to be given to an officer designated by me, the other to be retained by such officer or officers as you may designate. The officers to give their individual paroles not to take up arms against the Government of the United States until properly exchanged, and each company or regimental commander sign a like parole for the men of their commands. The arms, artillery and public property to be parked and stacked, and turned over to the officer appointed by me to receive them. This will not embrace the side-arms of the officers, not their private horses or baggage. This done, each officer and man will be allowed to return to their homes, not to be disturbed by United States authority so long as they observe their paroles and the laws in force where they may reside.

Very respectfully,

U. S. GRANT
Lt. Gen.

THOMAS JEFFERSON

Thomas Jefferson was a graduate of William & Mary College, an attorney, a member of the Virginia house of burgesses, a member of the Continental Congress, author of the Declaration of Independence, Governor of Virginia, minister to France, the first Secretary of State, the second Vice-President, the third President, and the founder of the University of Virginia, for which he wanted to be remembered particularly. His writings, mostly correspondence, are gathered in nineteen volumes, each of about 450 pages. These are titled, <u>The Writings of Thomas Jefferson</u>, and were issued in 1904 under the auspices of The Thomas Jefferson Memorial Association of the United States, Washington, D.C. The first three selections of Thomas Jefferson's writings shown here are found in these volumes.

Practically any document of Jefferson's would serve as a model of clear writing. It appears that Jefferson did not write in the informal style and was not known as a story teller. He differed from Lincoln on both counts. He is formal in his correspondence and his speeches. He can use lofty language when the occasion requires it, as in the Declaration of Independence.

The first selection is taken from Jefferson's first inaugural address, delivered March 4th, 1801. If this address is not clear on the first reading, there are two reasons. The first is that the choice of phrases has changed slightly in two centuries. The other is that ideas and political concepts that some speakers would discuss in a paragraph are said here in two or three words. The beauty of the speech reveals itself on the second reading.

> Equal and exact justice to men whatever state or persuasion, religious or political; peace, commerce and honest friendship with all nations, entangling alliances with none; the support of the State Governments in all their rights, as the most competent

administration for our domestic concerns, and the surest bulwarks against anti-republican tendencies; the preservation of the General Government in its whole constitutional vigor as the sheet anchor of our peace at home, and safety abroad; a jealous care of the right of election by the people—a mild and safe corrective of abuses, which are lopped by the sword of revolution, when peaceable remedies are unprovided; absolute acquiescence in the decision of the majority, the vital principle of republics from which there is no appeal but to force, the vital principle and immediate source of despotism; a well-disciplined militia, our best reliance in peace and for the first moments of war, till regulars may relieve them; the supremacy of the civil over the military authority; economy in the public expense that labor may be lightly burdened; the honest payment of our debts and sacred preservation of the public faith; encouragement of agriculture, and of commerce as its handmaid; the diffusing of information and the arraignment of all abuses at the bar of public reason; freedom of religion; freedom of the press; freedom of persons under the protection of the habeas corpus, and trial by juries impartially selected.

The second selection is a letter to Captain Meriwether Lewis, commanding officer of the Lewis & Clark Expedition. The purchase of the lands west of the Mississippi was being negotiated with Spain and France at the time the letter was written.

Washington, U.S. of A., July 4, 1803

Dear Sir,—In the journey you are about to undertake, for the discovery of the course and source of the Missouri, and the most convenient water communication from thence to the Pacific Ocean, your party being small, it is expected that you will encounter considerable dangers from the Indian inhabitants. Should you escape those dangers, and reach the Pacific Ocean, you may find it imprudent to hazard a return the same way, and be forced to seek a passage round by sea, in such vessels as you may find on the Western coast; but you will be without money, without clothes, and other necessaries, as a sufficient supply cannot be carried from hence. Your resource, in that case, can only be the credit of the United States; for which purpose I hereby authorize you to draw on the Secretaries of State, of the Treasury, of War, and of the Navy of the United States, according as you may find your draughts will be most negotiable, for yourself and men; and I solemnly pledge the faith of the United States, that these draughts shall be paid punctually at the date at which they are made payable. I also ask the consuls, agents, merchants, and citizens of any nation with which we have intercourse or amity, to furnish you with those supplies which your necessities may call for, assuring them of honorable and prompt retribution; and our own consuls in foreign parts, where you may happen to be, are hereby instructed and required to be aiding and assisting to you in whatsoever may be necessary for procuring your return back to the United States. And to give more entire satisfaction and confidence to those who may be disposed to aid you, I, Thomas Jefferson, President of the United States of America, have written this letter of general credit for you with my own hand, and signed it with my name.

The third selection is a letter to a friend in France. Jefferson was minister to France 1785-1789. At the time of writing this particular letter, Jefferson had eight months remaining in his second term as president. The letter demonstrates Jefferson's interest in many matters, agriculture among them. While the letter to Meriwether Lewis, above, is strictly business, this letter, though tending to business, exudes charm.

To Monsieur Sylvestre.
Washington, July 15, 1808

Sir,—I had received from you on a former occasion the four first volumes of the Memoirs of the Agricultural Society of the Seine, and since that, your letter of September 19th, with the 6th, 7th, 8th and 9th volumes, being the years 1804, '5, '6, with some separate memoirs. These I have read with great avidity and satisfaction, and now return you my thanks for them. But I owe particular acknowledgments for the valuable present of the Theatre de Serres, which I consider as a prodigy for the age in which it was composed, and shows an advancement in the science of agriculture which I had never suspected to have belonged to that time. Brought down to the present day by the very valuable notes added, it is really such a treasure of agricultural knowledge, as has not before been offered to the world in a single work.

It is not merely for myself, but for my country, that I must do homage to the philanthropy of the Society, which has dictated their destination for me of their newly improved plough. I shall certainly so use it as to answer their liberal views, by making the opportunities of profiting by it as general as possible.

I have just received information that a plough addressed to me has arrived at New York, from England, but unaccompanied by any letter or other explanation. As I have no intimation of such an article to be forwarded to me from that country, I presume it is the one sent by the Society of the Seine, that it has been carried into England under their orders of council, and permitted to come on from thence. This I shall know within a short time. I shall with great pleasure attend to the construction and transmission to the Society of a plough with mould-board. This is the only part of that useful instrument to which I have paid any particular attention. But knowing how much the perfection of the plough must depend, 1st, on the line of traction; 2d, on the direction of the share; 3d, on the angle of the wing; 4th, on the form of the mould-board; and persuaded that I shall find the three first advantages eminently exemplified in that which the Society sends me, I am anxious to see combined with these a mould-board of my form, in the hope it will still advance the perfection of that machine. But for this I must ask time till I am relieved from the cares which have now a right to all my time, that is to say, till next spring. Then giving, in the leisure of retirement, all the time and attention this construction merits and requires, I will certainly render to the Society the results in a plough of the best form I shall be able to have executed. In the meantime, accept for them and yourself the assurances of my high respect and consideration."

The fourth selection from Jefferson consists of three of the four inscriptions engraved on the interior walls of the Jefferson Memorial in

Washington, D.C. The fourth panel contains phrases from the Declaration of Independence.

> Almighty God hath created the mind free. All attempts to influence it by temporal punishments or burthens . . . are a departure from the plan of the Holy Author of our religion . . . No man shall be compelled to frequent or support any religious worship or ministry or shall otherwise suffer on account of his religious opinions or belief, but all men shall be free to profess and by argument to maintain, their opinions in matters of religion. I know but one code of morality for men whether acting singly or collectively." (From the Virginia Statute for Religious Freedom.)

> God who gave us life gave us liberty. Can the liberties of a nation be secure when we have removed a conviction that these liberties are the gift of God? Indeed I tremble for my country when I reflect that God is just, that his justice cannot sleep forever. Commerce between master and slave is despotism. Nothing is more certainly written in the book of fate than that these people are to be free. Establish the law for educating the common people. This is the business of the state to effect and on a general plan."

> I am not an advocate for frequent changes in laws and constitutions, but laws and institutions must go hand in hand with the progress of the human mind. As that becomes more developed, more enlightened, as new discoveries are made, new truths discovered and manners and opinions change, with the change of circumstances, institutions must advance also to keep pace with the times. We might as well require a man to wear still the coat which fitted him when a boy as civilized society to remain ever under the regimen of their barbarous ancestors.

ABRAHAM LINCOLN

Of our presidents, Abraham Lincoln may have been the most versatile speaker and writer. He was a member of the Illinois legislature, an attorney, a one-term member of the House of Representatives (1847-1849), and the unsuccessful candidate for the U.S. Senate against Stephen A. Douglas in 1858. He was elected the sixteenth president of the United States on the Republican ticket in November 1860 and re-elected in 1864.

Lincoln adapted his speech and writing to the occasion. He was a master story teller, a winning lawyer in front of a jury, a persuasive speaker in Congress who gave the rationale for his points of view while destroying, with relish and caustic humor, the arguments and reputations of others when the evidence made it necessary for him to do so.

The early speeches did not suggest that Lincoln would, in twenty years, develop extraordinary powers of persuasion in his addresses. When he wanted to, or when he had to, Lincoln could say and write the sort of stuff that ends up carved in marble on the inside walls of memorial buildings. He shares that power with Jefferson.

The first selection consists of excerpts from a speech given before the Young Men's Lyceum of Springfield, Illinois on January 27, 1838. The address is titled, The Perpetuation of our Political Institutions. It is taken from The Collected Works of Abraham Lincoln, Roy P. Basler, Editor; Rutgers University Press, New Brunswick, New Jersey, 1953.

> As a subject for the remarks of the evening, the perpetuation of our political institutions, is selected.

> In the great journal of things happening under the sun, we, the American People, find our account running, under date of the nineteenth century of the Christian era. We find ourselves

in the peaceful possession, of the fairest portion of the earth, as regards extent of territory, fertility of soil, and salubrity of climate. We find ourselves under the government of a system of political institutions, conducing more essentially to the ends of civil and religious liberty, than any of which the history of former times tells us. We, when mounting the stage of existence, found ourselves the legal inheritors of these fundamental blessings. We toiled not in the acquirement or establishment of them—they are a legacy bequeathed us, by a once hardy, brave, and patriotic, but now lamented and departed race of ancestors. Theirs was the task (and nobly they performed it) to possess themselves, and through themselves, us, of this goodly land; and to uprear upon its hills and its valleys, a political edifice of liberty and equal rights; 'tis ours only, to transmit these, the former, unprofaned by the foot of an invader; the latter, undecayed by the lapse of time, and untorn by usurpation—to the latest generation that fate shall permit the world to know. This task of gratitude to our fathers, justice to ourselves, duty to posterity, and love for our species in general, all imperatively require us faithfully to perform.

How, then, shall we perform it? At what point shall we expect the approach to danger? By what means shall we fortify against it? Shall we expect some transatlantic military giant, to step the Ocean, and crush us at a blow? Never! All the armies of Europe, Asia and Africa combined, with all the treasure of the earth (our own excepted) in their military chest; with a Buonaparte for a commander, could not by force, take a drink from the Ohio, or make a track on the Blue Ridge, in a trial of a thousand years.

At what point then is the approach of danger to be expected? I answer, if it ever reaches us, it must spring up amongst us. It cannot come from abroad. If destruction be our lot, we must ourselves be its author and finisher. As a nation of free men, we must live through all time, or die by suicide."

Lincoln, having introduced the topic, moves to the central theme, the increased incidence of mob rule. Here is one more paragraph:

Such are the effects of mob law; and such are the scenes, becoming more and more frequent in this land so lately famed for love of law and order; and the stories of which, have even now grown too familiar, to attract any thing more, than an idle remark.

The second selection is taken from the same book as above. Lincoln is speaking on the floor of the House of Representatives about Lewis Cass, senator from Michigan, who will become the candidate for president for the Democratic Party in the 1848 election. He lost to General Zachary Taylor. In the moments before the excerpt, Lincoln, having the floor, addresses the other side of the aisle, the Democrats, and teases them about running their last five presidential candidates on the coattails of Andrew Jackson.

We pick up Lincoln's words as he decides to tear into the Democrats over Lewis Cass, who, although he, Cass, was involved militarily in the War of 1812 and was Secretary of War under Jackson (1831-36), is not held in high esteem by Lincoln. The date is July 27, 1848. The segment is titled, <u>Military Tail of the Great Michigander</u>.

But in my hurry I was very near closing on the subject of military tails before I was done with it. There is one entire article of the sort I have not discussed yet; I mean the military tail you democrats are now engaged in dovetailing onto the great Michigander. Yes sir, all his biographers (and they are legion) have him in hand, tying him to a military tail, like so many mischievous boys tying a dog to a bladder of beans. True, the material they have is very limited; but they drive at it, might and main. He invaded Canada without resistance, and he <u>out</u>vaded it without pursuit. As he did both under orders, I suppose there was, to him, neither credit nor discredit in them; but they are made to constitute a large part of the tail. He was not at Hull's surrender, but he was close by; he volunteered to aid General Harrison on the day of the battle of the Thames; and, as you said in 1840, Harrison was picking huckleberries two miles off while the battle was fought; I suppose it is a just conclusion with you, to say Cass was aiding Harrison to pick huckleberries. This is about all, except the mooted question of the broken sword. Some authors say he broke it, some say he threw it away, and some others, who ought to know, say nothing about it. Perhaps it would be a fair historical compromise to say, if he did not break it, he didn't do any thing else with it.

By the way, Mr. Speaker, did you know I am a military hero? Yes sir; in the days of the Black Hawk war, I fought, bled, and came away. Speaking of General Cass' career, reminds me of my own. I was not at Stillman's defeat, but I was about as near it, as Cass was to Hull's surrender; and like him, I saw the place very soon afterwards. It is quite certain I did not break my sword, for I had none to break; but I bent a musket pretty badly on one occasion. If Cass broke his sword, the idea is, he broke it in desperation; I bent the musket by accident. If General Cass went in advance of me in picking huckleberries, I guess I surpassed him in charges upon the wild onions. If he saw any live, fighting Indians, it was more than I did; but I had a good many bloody struggles with the mosquitoes; and although I never fainted from the loss of blood, I can truly say I was often very hungry. Mr. Speaker, if I should ever conclude to doff whatever our democratic friends may suppose there is of black cockade federalism about me, and thereupon, they shall take me up as their candidate for the Presidency, I protest they shall not make fun of me, as they have of General Cass, by attempting to write me into a military hero."

The third selection is the open letter to Horace Greeley, editor of the New York Tribune. The sentiments expressed in the letter are less anti-slavery than one might expect. The Emancipation Proclamation, at least an early draft of it, may have been in Lincoln's desk drawer at the time this letter was written, but the Proclamation would not be made public until January 1, 1863. The confidence that Lincoln has in his views comes through in the strong, short, simple expression of his convictions.

Executive Mansion
Washington, August 22, 1862

Hon. Horace Greeley.

Dear Sir: I have just read yours of the 19th, addressed to myself through the New York Tribune. If there be in it any statements or assumptions of fact which I may know to be erroneous, I do not now and here controvert them. If there be any inferences which I may believe to be falsely drawn, I do not, now and here, argue against them. If there be perceptible in it an impatient and dictatorial tone, I wave it in deference to an old friend, whose heart I have always supposed to be right.

As to the policy I 'seem to be pursuing,' as you say, I have not meant to leave any one in doubt.

I would save the Union. I would save it the shortest way under the Constitution. The sooner the national authority can be restored, the nearer the Union will be 'the Union as it was.' If there be those who would not save the Union unless they could at the same time save slavery, I do not agree with them. If there be those who would not save the Union unless they could at the same time destroy slavery, I do not agree with them. My paramount object in this struggle is to save the Union, and not either to save or to destroy slavery. If I could save the Union without freeing any slave, I would do it; and if I could save it by freeing all the slaves, I would do it; and if I could save it by freeing some and leaving others alone, I would also do that. What I do about slavery and the colored race, I do because I believe it helps save the Union; and what I forebear, I forebear because I do not believe it would help save the Union. I shall do less whenever I shall believe what I am doing hurts the cause, and I shall do more whenever I shall believe doing more will help the cause. I shall try to correct errors when shown to be errors, and I shall adopt new views so fast as they shall appear to be true views.

I have here stated my purpose according to my view of official duty, and I intend no modification of my oft-expressed personal wish that all men, everywhere, could be free.

Yours,
A. Lincoln

THOMAS MACAULAY

How similar are the lives of Macaulay and Churchill! Perhaps one modeled his life after that of the other. Certainly Churchill read and studied Macaulay. Thomas Babington Macaulay, 1800-1859, was historian, essayist, member of the House of Commons, minister, government official in India, and at the end, member of the House of Lords. Had his life not been cut short by a weak heart, he would have added other accomplishments.

Macaulay's sister married a certain Trevelyan. They would produce historians bearing that name. It is she who collected her brother's complete works into eight volumes for publication in 1866. The son of this union, George Otto Trevelyan, published a biography of his uncle Thomas Macaulay in 1876.

Macaulay is remembered principally for the <u>History of England from the Accession of James II</u>. James II came to the throne in 1685, followed by William of Orange and Mary in 1688. The excerpt presented here is taken from the <u>History</u> and gives a sketch of the character of William, more properly known as William III. Little wonder Macaulay warms to the topic; while at Trinity College, Cambridge, he won a prize for an essay on the character of William III. The insight is precise, the selection of words and phrases excellent. Macaulay may hold the record for lengthy paragraphs placed one after the other. The purpose of keeping paragraphs short may be to make reading manageable. In place of short paragraphs, Macaulay gives us interesting topics in beautiful English. (The factual information above is taken from the Encyclopedia Britannica, Fourteenth Edition).

Here is the excerpt from the <u>History</u>, the beginning of Chapter VII.

The place which William Henry, Prince of Orange Nassau, occupies in the history of England and of mankind is so great that it may be desirable to portray with some minuteness the strong lineaments of his character.

He was now in his thirty-seventh year. But both in body and in mind he was older than other men of the same age. Indeed it might be said that he had never been young. His external appearance is almost as well known to us as to his own captains and counsellors. Sculptors, painters, and medalists exerted their utmost skill in the work of transmitting his features to posterity; and his features were such as no artist could fail to seize, and such as, once seen, could never be forgotten. His name at once calls up before us a slender and feeble frame, a lofty and ample forehead, a nose curved like the beak of an eagle, an eye rivalling that of an eagle in brightness and keenness, a thoughtful and somewhat sullen brow, a firm and somewhat peevish mouth, a cheek pale, thin, and deeply furrowed by sickness and by care. That pensive, severe, and solemn aspect could scarcely have belonged to a happy or a goodhumored man. But it indicates in a manner not to be mistaken capacity equal to the most arduous enterprises, and fortitude not to be shaken by reverses or dangers.

Nature had largely endowed William with the qualities of a great ruler; and education had developed those qualities in no common degree. With strong natural sense, and rare force of will, he found himself, when first his mind began to open, a fatherless and motherless child, the chief of a great but depressed and disheartened party, and the heir to vast and indefinite pretensions, which excited the dread and aversion of the oligarchy then supreme in the United Provinces. The common people, fondly attached during a century to his house, indicated, whenever they saw him, in a manner not to be mistaken, that they regarded him as their rightful head. The able and experienced ministers of the republic, mortal enemies of his name, came every day to pay their feigned civilities to him, and to observe the progress of his mind.

The first movements of his ambition were carefully watched; every unguarded word uttered by him was noted down; nor had he near him any adviser on whose judgment reliance could be placed. He was scarcely fifteen years old when all the domestics who were attached to his interest, or who enjoyed any share of his confidence, were removed from under his roof by the jealous government. He remonstrated with energy beyond his years, but in vain. Vigilant observers saw the tears more than once rise in the eyes of the young State prisoner. His health, naturally delicate, sank for a time under the emotions which his desolate situation had produced. Such situations bewilder and unnerve the weak, but call forth all the strength of the strong. Surrounded by snares in which an ordinary youth would have perished, William learned to tread at once warily and firmly. Long before he reached manhood he knew how to keep secrets, how to baffle curiosity by dry and guarded answers, how to conceal all passions under the same show of grave tranquillity. Meanwhile he made little proficiency in fashionable or literary accomplishments. The manners of the Dutch nobility of that age wanted the grace which was found in the highest perfection among the gentlemen of France, and which, in an inferior degree, embellished the Court of England; and his manners were altogether Dutch. Even his countrymen thought him blunt. To foreigners he often seemed churlish. In his intercourse with the world in general he appeared ignorant or negligent of those arts which double the value of a favour and take away the sting of a refusal. He was little interested in letters or science. The discoveries of Newton and Leibnitz, the poems of Dryden and Boileau, were unknown to him. Dramatic performances tired him; and he was glad to turn away from the stage and to talk about public affairs, while Orestes was raving, or Tartuffe was pressing Elmira's hand. He had indeed some talent for sarcasm, and not seldom employed, quite unconsciously, a natural rhetoric, quaint, indeed, but vigorous and original. He did not, however, in the least affect the character of a wit or of an orator. His attention had been confined to those studies which form strenuous and sagacious men of business. From a child he listened with interest when high questions of alliance, finance, and war were discussed. Of geometry he learned as much as was necessary for the construction of a ravelin or a hornwork. Of languages, by the help of a memory singularly powerful, he learned as much as enabled him to comprehend and answer without assistance everything that was said to him, and every letter which he received. The Dutch was his own tongue. He understood Latin, Italian, and Spanish. He spoke and wrote French, English, and German, inelegantly, it is true, and inexactly, but fluently and intelligibly. No qualification could be more important to a man whose life was to be passed in organizing great alliances, and in commanding armies assembled from different countries.

PLUTARCH

The Lives of Noble Grecians and Romans
Plutarch
Random House, Inc., The Modern Library Series

The following is taken from The Lives of Noble Grecians and Romans, by Plutarch (A.D. 46-120). The translation from the Latin is by John Dryden, the 17th Century English poet, playwright, and essayist. Julius Caesar has been murdered in the Senate in 44 B.C. These final paragraphs in the recounting of the life of Julius Caesar by Plutarch speak of the deaths of Cassius and Brutus at Philippi in 42 B.C.

Toward the end of the second paragraph, the text contains this sentence, " . . . he drew up his army near Philippi against Anthony and Caesar." This Caesar is not Julius, who has been dead two years, but Octavianus, Julius' great-nephew, who with Mark Anthony defeated the armies of Brutus and Cassius, ending the revenge against the murderers of Julius. Octavianus became Caesar Augustus in 27 B.C. Octavianus is known as well by the name Octavius.

> The most remarkable of mere human coincidences was that which befell Cassius, who, when he was defeated at Philippi, killed himself with the same dagger which he had made use of against Caesar. The most signal preternatural appearances were the great comet, which shone very bright for seven nights after Caesar's death, and then disappeared, and the dimness of the sun, whose orb continued pale and dull for the whole of that year, never showing its ordinary radiance at its rising, and giving but a weak and feeble heat. The air consequently was damp and gross

for want of stronger rays to open and rarify it. The fruits, for that reason, never properly ripened, and began to wither and fall off for want of heat before they were fully formed. But above all, the phantom which appeared to Brutus showed the murder was not pleasing to the gods. The story of it is this.

Brutus, being to pass his army from Abydos to the continent on the other side, laid himself down one night, as he used to do, in his tent, and was not asleep, but thinking of his affairs, and what events he might expect. For he is related to have been the least inclined to sleep of all men who have commanded armies, and to have had the greatest natural capacity for continuing awake, and employing himself without need of rest. He thought he heard a noise at the door of his tent, and looking that way, by the light of his lamp, which was almost out, saw a terrible figure, like that of a man, but of unusual stature and severe countenance. He was somewhat frightened at first, but seeing it neither did nor spoke anything to him, only stood silently by his bedside, he asked who it was. The specter answered him, "Thy evil genius, Brutus, thou shalt see me at Philippi." Brutus answered courageously, "Well, I shall see you," and immediately the appearance vanished. When time was come, he drew up his army near Philippi against Antony and Caesar, and in the first battle won the day, routed the enemy, and plundered Caesar's camp. The night before the second battle, the same phantom appeared to him again, but spoke not a single word. He presently understood his destiny was at hand, and exposed himself to all the dangers of the battle. Yet he did not die in the fight, but seeing his men defeated, got up to the top of a rock, and there presenting his sword to his naked breast, and assisted, as they say, by a friend, who helped him to give the thrust, met his death."

LEO TOLSTOY

War and Peace by Leo Tolstoy, written in 1864, re-published in 1942 as the Inner Sanctum Edition by Simon and Schuster, New York. The translation is by Louise and Aylmer Maude.

The event described in this passage occurs at the end of August, 1812. The Battle of Borodino has taken place and the Russian Army is retreating through Moscow. As the Rostov family prepares to leave the city, carts of wounded soldiers from Borodino go past the Rostov's house. Natasha, Count Rostov's daughter, is at the center of this episode. Page 951.

The voices and footsteps of the many servants and of the peasants who had come with the carts resounded as they shouted to one another in the yard and in the house. The count had been out since morning. The countess had a headache brought on by all the noise and turmoil and was lying down in the new sitting room with a vinegar compress on her head. Petya was not at home, he had gone to visit a friend with whom he meant to obtain a transfer from the militia to the active army. Sonya was in the ballroom looking after the packing of the glass and china. Natasha was sitting on the floor and holding in her hands the old ball dress (already out of fashion) which she had worn at her first Petersburg ball.

Natasha was ashamed at doing nothing when everyone else was so busy, and several times that morning had tried to set to work, but her heart was not in it, and she could not and did not know how to do anything except with all her heart and all her might. For a while she had stood beside Sonya while the china was being packed and tried to help, but soon gave it up and went to her room to pack her own things. At first she found it amusing to give away dresses and ribbons to the maids, but when that was done and what was left still had to be packed, she found it dull.

"Dunyasha, you pack! You will, won't you, dear?" And when Dunyasha willingly promised to do it all for her, Natasha sat down on the floor, took her old ball dress, and fell into a reverie quite unrelated to what ought to have occupied her thoughts now. She was roused from her reverie by the talk of the maids in the next room (which was theirs) and by the sounds of their hurried footsteps going back to the porch. Natasha got up and looked out the window. An enormously long row of carts full of wounded men had stopped in the street.

The housekeeper, the old nurse, the cooks, coachmen, maids, footmen, postilions, and scullions stood at the gate, staring at the wounded.

Natasha, throwing a clean pocket handkerchief over her hair and holding an end of it in each hand, went out into the street.

The former housekeeper, old Mavra Kuzminichna, had stepped out of the crowd by the gate, gone up to a cart with a hood constructed of bast mats, and was speaking to a pale young officer who lay inside. Natasha moved a few steps forward and stopped shyly, still holding her handkerchief, and listened to what the housekeeper was saying.

"Then you have nobody in Moscow?" she was saying. "You would be more comfortable somewhere in a house . . . in ours, for instance . . . the family are leaving."

"I don't know if it would be allowed," replied the officer in a weak voice. "Here is our commanding officer . . . ask him," and he pointed to a stout major who was walking back along the street past the row of carts.

Natasha glanced with frightened eyes at the face of the wounded officer and at once went to the major.

"May the wounded men stay in our house?" she asked.

The major raised his hand to his cap with a smile.

"Which one do you want, Ma'am'selle?" said he, screwing up his eyes and smiling.

Natasha quietly repeated her question, and her face and whole manner were so serious, though she was still holding the ends of her handkerchief, that the major ceased smiling and after some reflection—as if considering in how far the thing was possible—replied in the affirmative.

"Oh yes, why not? They may," he said.

With a slight inclination of her head, Natasha stepped back quickly to Mavra Kuzminichna, who stood talking compassionately to the officer. "They may. He says they may!" whispered Natasha.

CONCLUSION

Readers may reflect after finishing the text that the list of errors made commonly and the section containing samples of good prose are strange companions. Not so. Our point is that good writing is good because it employs the most effective among the options of usage and because it is rid of common errors. You may ask, and rightly so, why was there not a section containing mediocre prose riddled with the poor choices that we complain about? Show us your proof! There is no section containing mediocre prose for this reason: we would not print another's prose as an example of mediocre work. It is one thing to say "We think we know how," as we are saying in this text. It is quite another thing to say, "Here is a practitioner of the writing art caught in the act of malpractice."

While we will not provide samples of questionable prose whose authors are identified, you can find your own. Armed with this text and your newspaper, turn to the editorial page, turn to your favorite columnists, take pen in hand and start underlining. Locate the infinitives split by adverbs, find adverbs that would lend power if they were located toward the end of the sentence, catch them when they write "is going to have to lower taxes," when they could have written "must lower taxes." Cross out needless words, look for improper sequence, and nab them when they use the same phrase three times in one article. By these exercises in editing, readers who do not already know them will learn the elements of powerful prose.

ABOUT THE AUTHORS

Robert B. Stanton earned a Ph.D. at the University of Indiana, Bloomington. He taught for many years at the University of Washington in the English department and retired as an associate professor.

Frederic Weekes has a degree from the University of Pennsylvania in electrical engineering. He maintains that what he knows about grammar came from writing data sheets, catalogs, instruction manuals and sales letters over a career lasting more than forty years.